MW01701036

Explanation of & Contemplation Upon AL-FATIHAH

The Mother of the Book & Integral Aspect of the Prayer

Shaykh Salih ibn 'Abdul-'Aziz Alish-Shaykh

ISBN	:	979-8-3507-1154-7
First Edition	:	Shawwāl, 1444 A.H. / April 2023 C.E.
Cover Design	:	Aljadeed Design Co.
Translation by	:	Raha Batts

Publisher's Information:
Authentic Statements Publishing
5000 Locust St, Phila, Pa. 19139
215.382-3382 | 215.382.3782-Fax

Store:
5000 Locust St. (Side Entrance)
Phila Pa 19139
Website: www.authenticstatements.com
E-mail: Admin@authenticstatements.com

بسم الله الرحمن الرحيم

"In the Name of Allah, the Most Beneficent, the Ever Merciful"

المحتويات

Table of Contents

Transliteration Table

Consonants

ء	ʾ	د	d	ض	ḍ	ك	k
ب	b	ذ	dh	ط	ṭ	ل	l
ت	t	ر	r	ظ	ẓ	م	m
ث	th	ز	z	ع	ʿ	ن	n
ج	j	س	s	غ	gh	ه	h
ح	ḥ	ش	sh	ف	f	و	w
خ	kh	ص	ṣ	ق	q	ي	y

Vowels

Short	ـَ	a	ـِ	i	ـُ	u
Long	ـَا	ā	ـِي	ī	ـُو	ū
Diphthongs	ـَي	ay	ـَو	aw		

Arabic Glyphs & their meanings

صَلَّى ٱللَّهُ عَلَيْهِ وَسَلَّمَ May Allāh's praise & salutations be upon him	رَضِيَ ٱللَّهُ عَنْهُ May Allāh be pleased with him	رَضِيَ ٱللَّهُ عَنْهَا May Allāh be pleased with her
رَضِيَ ٱللَّهُ عَنْهُمْ May Allāh be pleased with them	سُبْحَانَهُ وَتَعَالَىٰ Glorified & Exalted is Allāh	عَزَّ وَجَلَّ (Allāh) the Mighty & Sublime
جَلَّ جَلَالُهُ (Allāh) His Majesty is Exalted	تَبَارَكَ وَتَعَالَىٰ (Allāh) the Blessed & Exalted	عَلَيْهِ ٱلسَّلَامُ Peace be upon Him
رَحِمَهُ ٱللَّهُ May Allāh have mercy on him	رَحِمَهُمُ ٱللَّهُ May Allāh have mercy upon them	حَفِظَهُ الله May Allāh preserve him

Introduction

The praise is for Allah, the One worthy of all praise and the possessor of all good and bounty. The praise is for Allah who possesses beautiful names and lofty attributes. The praise is for Allah who is worthy of the most complete forms of praise.

The praise is for Allah who has guided us to Islam and has granted us success upon the goodness that we are within; from holding fast to His Book and the Sunnah of His Messenger (صَلَّىٰ ٱللَّهُ عَلَيْهِ وَسَلَّمَ) as much as we are able. The praise is for Allah who is praised for (His) Excellence and He is praiseworthy in all circumstances.

I testify that none has the right to be worshiped in truth except Allah, alone, having no partners and I testify that Muhammad (صَلَّىٰ ٱللَّهُ عَلَيْهِ وَسَلَّمَ) is the servant of Allah and His Messenger; (he is) loved and his dear friend. May the prayers and peace of Allah be upon him, his family, and whoever follows their guidance until the Day of Recompense. To proceed:

I ask Allah, the Majestic and High, to make us and you from those who give due consideration to the Qur'an and who contemplate upon it; those who find it easy to read it, recite it, memorize it, reflect upon it, and understand it. I ask Him, the Majestic and High, to give us understanding of it such as will cool our eyes and give contentment to our souls. Moreover, the beginning of the Magnificent Qur'an is the Opening Chapter of the Book (Fatihah Al-Kitab); and the first of that which is explained from the Qur'an is the tremendous chapter. For its Tafsir—in addition to it being needed in order to understand seven verses from the Qur'an—it is likewise needed for the prayer—which is the greatest of the actions from the pillars of Islam. And the reward is only greatened for the one who reflects upon the Book of Allah that he is reciting and he says that which says within his prayer based upon knowledge, belief, and understanding.

✿✿✿

The Names of the Opening Chapter of the Book

Regarding the Opening Chapter of the Book, the Prophet (صَلَّى ٱللَّهُ عَلَيْهِ وَسَلَّمَ) named it, in that which is reported within the Sahih, the Magnificent Qur'an and the Seven Oft-Recited Verses. He (صَلَّى ٱللَّهُ عَلَيْهِ وَسَلَّمَ) said:

«فَاتِحَةُ الْكِتَابِ هي السَّبْعُ المَثانِي، والقُرْآنُ العَظِيمُ الذي أُوتِيتُهُ»

"The opening of the Book is the seven oft-repeated verses and the Magnificent Qur'an which I have been given."[1]

The Qur'an is commenced with the Opening Chapter of the Book. It is also called Umm Al-Qur'an (the Mother of the Qur'an) and Umm Al-Kitab (the Mother of the Book).[2] This

[1] Reported by Al-Bukhari within his Sahih in the Book of Tafsir; Chapter: What has Come regarding the Opening Chapter of the Book (no. 4474) from the Hadith of Abu Sa'id ibn Al-Ma'la. Refer to Fat'h Al-Bari (8/157)

[2] Refer to the speech regarding names of Al-Fatihah within Tafsir At-Tabari (1/105) as well as Majmu' Al-Fatawa (14/5), Jamal Al-Qurra' (1/176) and Tafsir At-Tahrir wat-Tanwir (1/131)

is because this book commences with it. Also, because the prayer is commenced with it. This reasoning was mentioned by Al-Bukhari within his Sahih. This is also due to the fact that all of the meanings of the Qur'an are embodied within this tremendous Surah; therefore, it is called the Mother of the Qur'an. This will be abundantly clear to you once you begin to understand it or after (studying) its explanation.

The Great Status of Al-Fatihah

Concerning this tremendous chapter, it is affirmed within the Sahih[1] that the Prophet (ﷺ) said:

«يَقُولُ قَالَ اللَّهُ تَعَالَى : قَسَمْتُ الصَّلَاةَ بَيْنِي وَبَيْنَ عَبْدِي نِصْفَيْنِ فَنِصْفُهَا لِي وَنِصْفُهَا لِعَبْدِي»

"Allah the Exalted has said: 'I have divided the prayer between me and my servant into two halves; half for me and half for my servant, and my servant shall have what he has asked for.'"

He intends by prayer, the *Opening Chapter of the Book.* Therefore, it is between the servant and his Lord within his prayer. This informs us of the great status of the Fatihah within the prayer. The Prophet (ﷺ) said:

---

[1] Reported by Muslim in the book of *Prayer*, chapter: *The Obligation of Reciting Al-Fatihah in Every Rak'ah* (no. 395) from the hadith of Abu Hurayrah (رَضِيَ اللَّهُ عَنْهُ). Refer, as well, to Majmu' Al-Fatawa (4/14) as well as Jamal Al-Qurra' (1/431).

«فَإِذَا قَالَ الْعَبْدُ: ﴿الْحَمْدُ لِلَّهِ رَبِّ الْعَالَمِينَ﴾ ، قَالَ اللَّهُ تَعَالَى: حَمِدَنِي عَبْدِي، وَإِذَا قَالَ: ﴿الرَّحْمَنِ الرَّحِيمِ﴾ ، قَالَ اللَّهُ تَعَالَى: أَثْنَى عَلَيَّ عَبْدِي، وَإِذَا قَالَ: ﴿مَالِكِ يَوْمِ الدِّينِ﴾ ، قَالَ: مَجَّدَنِي عَبْدِي - وَقَالَ مَرَّةً فَوَّضَ إِلَيَّ عَبْدِي - فَإِذَا قَالَ: ﴿إِيَّاكَ نَعْبُدُ وَإِيَّاكَ نَسْتَعِينُ﴾ قَالَ: هَذَا بَيْنِي وَبَيْنَ عَبْدِي، وَلِعَبْدِي مَا سَأَلَ، فَإِذَا قَالَ: ﴿اهْدِنَا الصِّرَاطَ الْمُسْتَقِيمَ صِرَاطَ الَّذِينَ أَنْعَمْتَ عَلَيْهِمْ غَيْرِ الْمَغْضُوبِ عَلَيْهِمْ وَلَا الضَّالِّينَ﴾ قَالَ : هَذَا لِعَبْدِي وَلِعَبْدِي مَا سَأَلَ»

"Allah has said: 'So when the servant says: 'All the praise is for Allah, Lord of all that exists' Allah, the Exalted says: 'My servant has praised me.' And when the servant says: 'The Most Merciful, the Bestower of Mercy' Allah the Exalted says: 'My servant has extolled me.' And when the servant says: 'Master of the Day of Judgment,' Allah says: 'My servant has glorified me.' And when he says: 'You alone we worship and you alone we ask for help.' Allah says: 'This is between me and my servant and my servant shall have whatever he has asked for.' And when he says: 'Guide us to the straight path, the path upon those whom you bestowed your Grace not the path of those whom have earned your anger, nor those who have gone astray.' Allah says: 'This is between Me and My servant and My servant shall have what he has asked for.'"

This, which this hadith has described, no doubt brings about understanding of this chapter and understanding of its meaning and contemplation upon its verses. As the poet said:

«فَلَيسَ سَواءً عالِمٌ وَجَهولُ»

"The one who knows and the ignorant are not equal."

He who recites these verses from Al-Fatihah, understanding their meaning, and comprehending its implications along with the recitation of his tongue is not equal with the one who utters something upon his tongue while his heart is distracted, or he is ignorant of it. How great is the prayer in terms of consultation with Allah the Mighty and Majestic by way of this tremendous chapter. This chapter is the opening chapter of the book and it is also the seven often recited verses as the Prophet (ﷺ) has mentioned within this hadith. And by way of it the statement of Allah the Exalted has explained:

﴿وَلَقَدْ آتَيْنَاكَ سَبْعًا مِّنَ الْمَثَانِي وَالْقُرْآنَ الْعَظِيمَ ﴿٨٧﴾﴾

"And We have certainly given you, [O Muhammad], seven of the often repeated [verses] and the great Qur'an." (Al-Hijr 15:87)

Hence the seven often recited verses are explained as being Al-Fatihah as the Prophet (ﷺ) has mentioned. Similarly, the tremendous Quran along with the seven often recited verses together have been explained as being the opening chapter of the book, as has preceded within the hadith of Abu Sa'id ibn Al-Mu'alla (رَضِيَ اللَّهُ عَنْهُ) which is reported by Al-Bukhari and other than him.

Beginning with the Seeking of Refuge and the Basmalah when Reciting Al-Fatihah

Concerning the phrase: I seek refuge with Allah from the accursed Shaytan; This chapter begins with the Basmalah and that which Allah, the Mighty and Majestic, has commanded the reader to do is to begin his recitation with the seeking of refuge with Allah from the accursed Shaytan. Therefore, it is binding upon him to understand and to know the meaning of the seeking of refuge with Allah, the Mighty and Majestic, from the accursed Shaytan. Allah, the Exalted, has said:

﴿فَإِذَا قَرَأْتَ الْقُرْآنَ فَاسْتَعِذْ بِاللَّهِ مِنَ الشَّيْطَانِ الرَّجِيمِ ﴿٩٨﴾﴾

"So when you recite the Qur'an, [first] seek refuge in Allah from Shaytan (Satan), the expelled [from His mercy]." (An-Nahl 16:98)

✿✿✿

The Wording of the Seeking of Refuge

The one who recites the Quran within the prayer and outside of the prayer is to begin with the statement:

«أَعُوذُ بِاللهِ مِنَ الشَّيطَانِ الرّجِيمِ»

"I seek refuge with Allah from the accursed Shaytan."

And if he were to add an attribute from the attributes of Allah the Exalted in order to display veneration for Him and exaltation of Him, then there is no harm. Such as one saying:

«أَعُوذُ بِاَللَّهِ السَّمِيعِ الْعَلِيمِ مِنْ الشَّيْطَانِ الرَّجِيمِ»

"I seek refuge with Allah the All-Hearing and the All-Knowing from the accursed Shaytan."

For ignorance is not attributed to Him. This is what has come within the sunnah, and all of those wordings have come from Him as has been stated by Ash-Shatibi:[1] "And if

[1] Within Haraz Al-Amani (pg. 8) and the completion of the line is: *"Based upon what has come being reported in Surah An-Nahl and if you were*

you were to add a statement absolving your Lord of imperfections then you are not accused of ignorance."

Meaning, if you were to add some of the various types of attributes of, Allah such as your saying:

«أَعُوذُ بِاللَّهِ السَّمِيعِ الْعَلِيمِ مِنْ الشَّيْطَانِ الرَّجِيمِ»

"I seek refuge with Allah the All-Hearing and the All-Knowing from the accursed Shaytan."[1]

And if one were to say:

«أَعُوذُ بِاللَّهِ الْحَيِّ الْقَيُّومِ مِنَ الشَّيْطَانِ الرَّجِيمِ»

"I seek refuge with Allah the Ever-Living the one who sustains and protects all that exist from the accursed Shaytan,"

You cannot be accused of ignorance and all of them are good and are considered to be from following the sunnah and are suitable. Hence, we have two descriptions that have come in this regard. The first is that one says: *I seek refuge with Allah from the accursed Shaytan.[2]* This is that which has come similarly within the Quran.

---

to add a statement absolving your lord of imperfections then you cannot be accused of ignorance."

[1] This has been reported by the compilers of the four Sunan books as well as Ahmad on the authority of Abu Sa'id Al-Khudri (رَضِيَ اللَّهُ عَنْهُ) with a good chain of narration. At-Tirmidhi said: *"It is the most famous hadith that has come in this regard."*

[2] This is that which is more suitable and it is that which the jurist have taken to. Such as, Abu Hanifah, Ash-Shafi'i, Ahmad and the texts of the two sahihs and other than them have come indicating this.

The second; is that which is affirmed within the sunnah; and it is:

«أَعُوذُ بِاللَّهِ السَّمِيعِ الْعَلِيمِ مِنَ الشَّيْطَانِ الرَّجِيمِ، مِنْ هَمْزِهِ، وَنَفْخِهِ، وَنَفْثِهِ»

"I seek refuge with Allah the All-Hearing the All-Knowing from the accursed Shaytan; from his hamzh همزه, his nafkh نفخه and his nafth نفثه.[1]"

The hamzh of Shaytan refers to his driving of a person insane. It is a type of illness that afflicts people driving them to insanity. The nafkh (blowing) of Shaytan refers to his arrogance. And the nafth of Shaytan refers to his poetry with which he intends falsehood. This is from that which is affirmed within the sunnah.

✪✪✪

[1] This has been reported by Abu Dawud within his Sunan in the book of Prayer, Chapter: *He Who Holds That the Prayer Should Be Commenced With Glorified be You, O Allah and the Praise be to you* (no. 775) and At-Tirmidhi within his Jami' in the book of Prayer upon the Prophet (صَلَّى ٱللَّهُ عَلَيْهِ وَسَلَّمَ), chapter: *What He Would Say When Commencing the Prayer.* (no. 242) from the hadith of Abu Sa'id Al-Khudri (رَضِيَ ٱللَّهُ عَنْهُ). See, as well, An-Nashr Fi Al-Qiraa'at Al-'Ashr (1/251).

The Meaning of the Isti'adhah (Seeking of Refuge)

The one who recites the Quran says: *"I seek refuge with Allah from the accursed Shaytan."* The meaning of: *"I seek refuge,"* is: I seek the protection of and I turn to for refuge, and beseech for protection with Allah, who is my true object of worship besides whom I worship no other. Nor do I entrust my affair to anyone other than Him. *"From..."* the evil of, *"the accursed Shaytan."* The one who has been repelled, cursed, distanced, and expelled from the mercy of Allah, the Majestic and High from amongst the devils of jinn and the devils of mankind that they should afflict me with harm within myself or harm deficiency within my religion or that they should afflict me in my steadfastness to the command of my Lord, or that they should turn me towards that which my God, my Patron Lord whom I worship does not like. Allah, the Exalted, has said:

﴿وَقُل رَّبِّ أَعُوذُ بِكَ مِنْ هَمَزَاتِ الشَّيَاطِينِ ﴿٩٧﴾
وَأَعُوذُ بِكَ رَبِّ أَن يَحْضُرُونِ ﴿٩٨﴾﴾

“And say, "My Lord, I seek refuge in You from the incitements of the devils, And I seek refuge in You, my Lord, lest they be present with me.” (Al-Mu’minun 23:97-98)

Likewise, Allah the Exalted has said:

﴿قُلْ أَعُوذُ بِرَبِّ الْفَلَقِ ۝١﴾

Say: “I seek refuge (with Allāh) the Lord of the daybreak.” (Al-Falaq 113:1)

Likewise, Allah has said:

﴿قُلْ أَعُوذُ بِرَبِّ النَّاسِ ۝١﴾

Say: “I seek refuge with (Allāh) the Lord of Mankind.” (An-Nas 114:1)

The meaning of all of this is: *I betake myself to, seek protection from, resort to Allah from the evil of Shaytan that he should afflict me* with something that is similar to what I have described. Hence, the meaning of *Al-‘Iyadh* العياذ is seeking refuge with, taking protection and precaution with Allah. So bear in mind when you say, “I take refuge” the meaning of that is that you are freeing your heart in the removal of evil from yourself, from everything other than Allah, the Majestic and High, and you know that the one who can repel the evil of Shaytan and the devils of Jinn and Mankind from you is none other than Allah, the Majestic and High.

When you say: “I seek refuge with Allah from the accursed Shaytan,” it is said while reciting that when the reciter recites the Qur’an Shaytan is present during that recital seeking to distract him from contemplating upon the verses in order that he can whisper to him and make him such that he is not mindful of what he is reciting. All of this and its like are from the evils of Shaytan whom Allah's refuge is being sought from. When one says: "I seek refuge with Allah," ***with Allah*** means with the true object of worship, the one besides whom there is no true object of worship. He is my object of worship whom I worship and whom I devote all of my worship to. This comprises the meaning of Lordship being devoted to Him who I entrust my affairs to and I place my reliance upon and seek protection from and I seek goodness from. And I seek from him distance from all evil and this is Allah in whose Hand is the dominion of all things.

✪✪✪

Seeking Refuge with Other Than Allah is Shirk

So one saying: "I seek refuge with Allah from the accursed Shaytan." The One with whom refuge is sought is Allah, the Majestic and High, alone and seeking refuge is an act of worship. However, it is an act of worship with the heart and shall not be devoted to anyone other than Allah, the Majestic and High. Therefore, it is not permissible to seek refuge with other than Allah, the Majestic and High, and whoever seeks refuge with other than Allah has committed polytheism. This is because Allah, the Majestic and High, is the One who protects from evil and He is the one who brings about goodness and prevents harm. Allah, the Majestic and High, has said:

﴿وَإِن يَمْسَسْكَ ٱللَّهُ بِضُرٍّ فَلَا كَاشِفَ لَهُۥٓ إِلَّا هُوَ ۖ وَإِن يَمْسَسْكَ بِخَيْرٍ فَهُوَ عَلَىٰ كُلِّ شَىْءٍ قَدِيرٌ ﴿١٧﴾﴾

"And if Allah should touch you with adversity, there is no remover of it except Him. And if He touches you with good - then He is over all things competent." (Al-An'am 6:17)

Likewise, Allah the Majestic and High said in another verse:

﴿وَإِن يَمْسَسْكَ اللَّهُ بِضُرٍّ فَلَا كَاشِفَ لَهُ إِلَّا هُوَ ۖ وَإِن يُرِدْكَ بِخَيْرٍ فَلَا رَادَّ لِفَضْلِهِ ۚ يُصِيبُ بِهِ مَن يَشَاءُ مِنْ عِبَادِهِ ۚ وَهُوَ الْغَفُورُ الرَّحِيمُ ﴿١٠٧﴾﴾

"And if Allah should touch you with adversity, there is no remover of it except Him; and if He intends for you good, then there is no repeller of His bounty. He causes it to reach whom He wills of His servants. And He is the Forgiving, the Merciful." (Yunus 10:107)

Likewise, Allah the Exalted has said:

﴿مَّا يَفْتَحِ اللَّهُ لِلنَّاسِ مِن رَّحْمَةٍ فَلَا مُمْسِكَ لَهَا ۖ وَمَا يُمْسِكْ فَلَا مُرْسِلَ لَهُ مِن بَعْدِهِ ۚ وَهُوَ الْعَزِيزُ الْحَكِيمُ ﴿٢﴾﴾

"Whatever Allah grants to people of mercy - none can withhold it; and whatever He withholds - none can release it thereafter. And He is the Exalted in Might, the Wise." (Fatir 35:2)

Therefore, the One who repels evil from His servant is Allah, the Majestic and High, and the One who brings about goodness for the servant is Allah, the Majestic and High. And the most evil of the people of evil upon the believing servant is the accursed Shaytan who is Iblis and his army amongst jinn and mankind. This is because the loftiest and most valuable of that which the believing servant has in this life is his being steadfast upon Islam. It is not possible to remain steadfast upon Islam unless one has protection and is safeguarded from the evils which afflict him in that and which the devils amongst mankind and the jinn utilize to transgress against him. Therefore, let the person take refuge with Allah from the accursed Shaytan.

✪✪✪

The Meaning of Shaytan in the Arabic Language

The people of knowledge say that Shaytan is taken from the word *Ash-Shatan* الشطن which means distance; because Shaytan in the Arabic language is applied to the one who is distant from goodness. So, everything that is distant from goodness is called a Shaytan;[1] or one who is distant from that which those of his genus are upon. Due to this it is said

[1] Al-Fuyumi said within Al-Misbah Al-Munir, under the definition of Shatana شطن, "Regarding Shaytan there are two statements. The first is that it is from the word Shatana, when one is distant from the truth or distant from the mercy of Allah thus the ن is one of its root letters and its pattern is فيعال. It refers to every evil and obstinate individual amongst jinn, mankind and animals. Thus, it is a Shaytan. A Bedouin described his horse saying, 'It is as if it is a Shaytan في أشطان.' The second statement is that the ي is one of its foundational letters and the ن is additional. This is an opposition to the first statement. Thus, it is from شاط/يشيط when one is upon falsehood or one burns. Its pattern is فعلان

regarding Iblis that he was a Shaytan. If the term Ash-Shaytan is used within the legislation, then Iblis is the foremost to enter into it. Meaning, Ash-Shaytan encompasses the devils amongst mankind and the devils amongst jinn. This is because the devils amongst mankind are distanced from goodness. Similarly, the devils amongst jinn are, likewise, distanced from goodness. From that which indicates this, as the scholars of tafsir have said, is the statement of the poet:

«أَيُّمَا شَاطِنٍ عَصَاهُ عُكَّاهُ... ثُمَّ يُلْقَى فِي السِّجْنِ وَالْأَغْلَالِ»

"Whenever a criminal disobeys his command;
He is tossed into imprisonment and shackles."

This phrase: "Whenever a *Shatin...*" (i.e., criminal, meaning one who is distant.) Therefore, Ash-Shaytan refers to distance. It is said as well that some animals are called Shaytan. This is in reference to their distance either from other animals of their species or their being distant from goodness. It is affirmed within Sahih Muslim.[1] From the hadith of Abu Dharr (رَضِيَ اللَّهُ عَنْهُ) that the Prophet (صَلَّى اللَّهُ عَلَيْهِ وَسَلَّمَ) said:

«اَلْكَلْبُ اَلْأَسْوَدِ شَيْطَانٌ»

"The black dog is Shaytan."

It is likewise affirmed that the Prophet (صَلَّى اللَّهُ عَلَيْهِ وَسَلَّمَ) saw someone following a pigeon and he said:

«شَيْطَانٌ يَتْبَعُ شَيْطَانَةً»

---

[1] In the Book of *Prayer*, Chapter: *The Distanced One Can Be from His Sutrah* (no.510)

"A Shaytan following another Shaytan."[1]

It is likewise affirmed from the hadith of Ibn Wahab (رَحِمَهُ ٱللَّهُ) with a sahih chain of narration that Umar was brought a horse that was not from those of the Arabs and he rode it and he saw it walking in a strange manner and it continued walking in this strange manner. Umar descended from it and said: *"You have not made me to ride except upon a Shaytan."[2]*

Therefore, Shaytan in the origin of the language is applied to the one that is distanced from goodness or distant from that which others of its species are upon. This is the general meaning. Thereafter, we returned to a specific meaning, and it is that Shaytan is the one that is distanced from goodness and described with evil. The Shaytan may be distanced from goodness in totality such as Iblis and those who follow him from his progeny and perhaps it is distanced from certain types of goodness but not in totality and this refers to those who have become a Shaytan from amongst mankind. Due to this, Allah the Mighty and Majestic and High is commanded with seeking refuge; that the person should seek refuge from the evils of Shaytan. He said:

---

[1] Reported by Abu Dawud within his Sunan in the Book of Manners, Chapter: Regarding Playing with Pigeons. (no.4940) from the hadith of Abu Hurayrah (رَضِيَ ٱللَّهُ عَنْهُ).

[2] Refer to Tafsir At-Tabari (1/109). As well as Tafsir ibn Kathir (1/115) who said concerning it that its chain of narration is sahih and the Birdhun amongst the horses is that which is not from amongst the Arabs. It is large in size. Refer to Taj Al-Arus.

﴿وَإِمَّا يَنزَغَنَّكَ مِنَ الشَّيْطَانِ نَزْغٌ فَاسْتَعِذْ بِاللَّهِ ۚ إِنَّهُ سَمِيعٌ عَلِيمٌ ﴿٢٠٠﴾﴾

"And if an evil suggestion comes to you from Satan, then seek refuge in Allah. Indeed, He is All- Hearing and All- Knowing." (Al-A'raf 7:200)

And this is within a number of verses. Hence, the servant is in dire need of seeking refuge with Allah, the Majestic and High, from Shaytan because Shaytan plots against the son of Adam with various types of schemes and he plots for him to harm him in his body and to harm him in his heart, and to harm him in his family, and to harm him in his wealth with various types of harm. Shaytan is not seen and his plots if he is amongst the Jinn are likewise not seen and if he is amongst mankind then they plot against the believers and they plot against their enemies. Also, none can protect from all of this except Allah, the Majestic and High. He is the one who, in reality, provides protection. As Allah has said:

﴿قَالَ لَا عَاصِمَ الْيَوْمَ مِنْ أَمْرِ اللَّهِ إِلَّا مَن رَّحِمَ ۚ﴾

"There is no protector today from the decree of Allah, except for whom He gives mercy." (Hud 11:43)

✿✿✿

The Meaning of Ar-Rajim (Cursed) Within the Arabic Language

This Shaytan, its description has come here wherein one says: "Ar-Rajim (cursed)." Therefore, one has sought refuge with Allah from the accursed Shaytan and the meaning of cursed is Al-Marjum (the one that has been expelled). The origin of Ar-Rajim in the Arabic language is tossing; either by way of statements or by actions. Ar-Ramy, as well is the meaning of killing for example or suspicion or a statement without evidence or proof. All of these meanings have come within the Quran. Allah has said:

﴿لَئِن لَّمْ تَنتَهِ لَأَرْجُمَنَّكَ ۖ﴾

"If you do not desist, I will surely (toss) stones (at) you." (Maryam 19:46)

Likewise, Allah the Exalted has said:

﴿رَجْمًا بِالْغَيْبِ﴾

"Guessing at the unseen;" (Al-Kahf 18:22)

Meaning, guessing at the unseen. This is from the statements regarding it. From that as well is the statement of the poet:

«وَمَا هُوَ عَنْهَا بِالحَدِيثِ المُرَجَّمِ»

"And he does not have anything against her except suspicious speech."[1]

The meaning of this is that which is a supposition having no evidence. The origin of the statement, "From the accursed Shaytan," means that the one who has been cursed and distanced from goodness, and Rajim bears the meaning of Rajum meaning he has been cursed and distanced from all good.

✡✡✡

[1] This is only one half of the line of poetry. The other line says, "*And war is not except that which you know and have tasted...*" It is from those lines that have been attributed to Zuhair ibn Abu Salma and the line is in Lisan Al-Arab (12/228). And in this line Ibn Al-Murajam as well as Rajam which is to falsely accuse someone without any proof only supposition. See as well Ad-Dhar Al-Masun (1/12)

Alert and Caution from the Whispers of the Accursed Shaytan

Once you know that this is the description of Shaytan and that he is distanced from goodness and that the servant who seeks refuge with Allah and recites this tremendous chapter and commences the recitation of the Qur'an desiring goodness, devoting himself to it, then let him be on guard from this Shaytan which bears this description of being cursed and distanced from goodness and expelled from the mercy of Allah, the Majestic and High. Without doubt this varies with the variation of the people. Shaytan afflicts each of the believers with some type of affliction except for those whom Allah keeps safe. So when the servant recites he bears this in mind and seeks protection and refuge with Allah. He seeks to be safeguarded by Allah from this Shaytan who is his enemy. For the enmity of Shaytan for the children of Adam is always at the forefront of the believer's mind. When he knows this then he has the strength to protect himself and safeguard himself by the bounty of Allah, the Majestic and High, from the prodding of the devil. This is because he is always taking refuge with Allah, the Majestic and High, from the accursed Shaytan.

﴿بِسْمِ ٱللَّهِ ٱلرَّحْمَٰنِ ٱلرَّحِيمِ﴾

In the Name of Allah the Most-Merciful, the Bestower of Mercy

Is the Basmalah a verse? Allah the Glorified says at the beginning of the Quran:

﴿بِسْمِ ٱللَّهِ ٱلرَّحْمَٰنِ ٱلرَّحِيمِ ١﴾

"In the Name of Allāh, the Most-Merciful (to His creation), the Bestower of Mercy." (Al-Fatihah 1:1)

This is a verse; and the people of knowledge have several statements regarding this.[1] However, that which is correct is that it is a verse that is recited at the beginning of every chapter of the Qur'an in order to separate between its chapters. Hence, it is a verse of the Quran and it is not a verse within every chapter and it is a portion within a verse within Surah An-Naml the statement of Allah the Exalted:

﴿إِنَّهُ مِن سُلَيْمَانَ وَإِنَّهُ بِسْمِ اللَّهِ الرَّحْمَٰنِ الرَّحِيمِ ٣٠﴾

---

[1] In this issue refer to *Majmu Al-Fatawa* by Ibn Taymiyyah (22/438 and 440). As well as Tafsir Ibn Kathir (1/116-117). As well as Nasr Al-Rayah (1/323 and 362). Ibn Jazri said within An-Nashr fi al-Qira'at al-'Ashr (1/271) after citing the differences of opinion between the scholars in this issue, "These statements are either negations or affirmations. That which we hold is that all of them are correct and that each of them bears truth. Hence, the difference within it is similar to the different recitations." This is excellent in exemplary speech.

"Indeed, it is from Sulayman (Solomon), and indeed, it reads: 'In the name of Allah, the Most-Merciful, the Bestower of Mercy." (An-Naml 27:30)

And it is not a verse at the beginning of Surah Al-Bara'a (Surah At-Tawbah).

✿✿✿

The meaning of: In the name of Allah, the Most Merciful, the Bestower of Mercy:

The Qur'an is commenced with it and the Basmalah is from the greatest of that which Allah has blessed the believers with in general, from the followers of the messengers. Because within it and by way of it there comes about the attainment of good, the full extent of which only Allah knows. Its general explanation is that the reciter of the book of Allah is saying: *"I recite the Qur'an seeking the help of every Name from the Names of my true object of worship, Allah, who is referred to as being the Most Merciful, the Bestower of Mercy; within whom the attribute of mercy is perfected and its effects are tremendous."* Therefore, he recites, and he reads seeking the help of Allah, the Majestic and High, utilizing every name from the names of Allah, the Majestic and High, using that as a means of nearness to Allah, the Majestic and High, by way of every Name from amongst his Names. You will know that when the knowledge of the beautiful names along with the attributes of Allah intensifies within His servant he bears this in mind when he says this speech;

when he mentions the tremendous names of Allah, the Majestic and High, and he will think about their effects. Meaning, he will bear their effects within the universe of Allah in mind and this will have an effect upon his heart bringing about various types of knowledge and various types of love and various types of good thoughts about Allah and various types of trust and reliance upon Allah the Majestic and High. All of this is appropriate to bear in mind when one begins with: *"In the name of Allah, the Most Merciful, the Bestower of Mercy."*

Clarifying the Connection Between the Preposition and the Prepositional Clause Within the Basmalah:

The scholars have said the preposition and the prepositional clause within the phrase: *Bismillah* has a connection inevitably either to a verb or a Masdar or something which bears the meaning of a verb. Some of the people of knowledge have determined it to be a latent Masdar[1]. Meaning: my beginning is in the Name of Allah or my recitation is with the name of Allah. This is because there comes within the Qur'an being connected to a preposition and a prepositional clause within the phrase *Bismillah*. Meaning, in the Name of Allah; this is within His statement in Surah Hud:

﴿وَقَالَ ارْكَبُوا فِيهَا بِسْمِ اللَّهِ مَجْرَاهَا وَمُرْسَاهَا ۚ إِنَّ رَبِّي لَغَفُورٌ رَّحِيمٌ ﴿٤١﴾﴾

[1] This is the view of the scholars of Basrah

And Nuh [Noah] said, "Embark therein; in the name of Allah is its course and its anchorage. Indeed, my Lord is Forgiving and Merciful." (Hud 11:41)

Therefore, within this verse the preposition and the prepositional clause came to be connected to the noun. Others have stated - and this is the most correct and strongest viewpoint - that it is connected to a (latent) verb.[1] And the verb is that which is appropriate in that instance. So, if the reciter begins by saying Bismillah before he recites then the latent phrase is: *"I read in the Name of Allah."* As is the case in the first of that which was revealed from the Qur'an wherein Allah said, **"(Iqra, meaning Read!)"** He said: "Read in the Name of the One who has created you."

﴿اقْرَأْ بِاسْمِ رَبِّكَ الَّذِي خَلَقَ ①﴾

"Recite (what is being revealed to you, O Muḥammad) by (commencing with) the name of your Lord Who created (all things)." (Alaq 96:1)

Hence, one is saying: *I recite in the name of Allah,* or: *I read in the name of Allah;* and the meaning of that is: I am reciting and reading, seeking the aid and utilizing as a means of nearness to Allah every Name that belongs to Allah, the Majestic and High.

✪✪✪

---

[1] This is the view of the scholars of Kufah. Refer to the details of this issue within Tafsir At-Tabari (1/112 and 116). As well as Ad-Darr Al-Masun (1/22-23)

The Meaning of Bismillah

Some of the people of knowledge hold that it means: By Allah. However, this is not a good viewpoint. Rather, what is correct is that what enters into this is all of Allah's Names because the (specific) name was left unmentioned. Therefore, it is correct to apply the phrase Bismillah to mean all of the beautiful names of Allah, the Majestic and High, and this has an effect upon the soul of the reciter. From amongst the people there are those who bear this in mind when they recite some of the names of Allah. And from amongst the people there are those who will call to mind other names which the first person did not bear in mind. All of this opens the heart within various types of worship and perhaps the people are variant in that. This is from that which should be their intent and from that which should be the case as it relates to them. For example, the reciter of the Quran and perhaps to be within a state of distress and will call to mind the names of Allah the Majestic and High which indicate relief from the stress. He will bear them in mind unintentionally. Due to this we find that the one who worships Allah the Majestic and High for hopes for His mercy calls to mind the names of Allah which have within them all types of beauty as Allah is described with and the one who is a sinner will call to mind that which contains majesty, and this is general for all of Allah's names. Due to this we say, then what is correct is that the statement, "Bismillah" is not specific to any one name and the latent meaning is not by Allah and the word اسم is not extra in order to emphasize the speech that has been mentioned. Rather, the meaning is I recite seeking nearness to Allah or seeking the help of every name that belongs to Allah the Majestic and High.[1]

✿✿✿

[1] Refer to Madarij Al-Salikin (1/89)

The Meaning of the Majestic Term 'Allah'

In the phrase Bismillah, I want to say regarding the term Allah adding to it that this term is that which is differed about and I will mention its details here because of its importance in creed. The verifiers from the people of knowledge say regarding the phrase Allah, that this is the greatest of the names of Allah, the Majestic and High. Its meaning is that it is a proper name for the One that is worshiped in truth. Hence, the other gods that are worshiped alongside Allah are not worshiped in truth. The true object of worship is Allah, the Majestic and High, alone without any partners. Therefore, the majestic term is a proper name of the One that is worshiped in truth.[1]

What is correct is that it is a derived term and it is not an underived term.[2] Its origin is *Al-Ilah* and the hamza was lightened over time thus it came to be Allah due to the

[1] Refer to Dar Al-Maslul (1/23), as well as Tafsir ibn Kathir (1/122)

[2] Refer to Tafsir At-Tabari (1/121), as well as Dar Al-Maslul (1/24) and Tafsir ibn Kathir (1/123-124), as well as At-Tahrir Wal Tanwir (1/163)

abundance of its usage at the beginning of the life of mankind. This is because shirk and taking other deities alongside Allah occurred after that. Since its origin is Al-Ilah then its pattern is فعال bearing the meaning of مفعول (an object). Meaning, that it bears the meaning of مألوه (the one that is deified upon). Just as Firash فراش bears the meaning of ma'frush مفروش and Wita' وطاء bears the meaning of mawtu' موطوء and the likes of this.

The term fi'al bearing the meaning of maf'ul occurs much within the Arabic language, as is well known. And the one that deified (المألوه) is a noun for the one that is deified in truth. It is extracted from أله/يأله/إلاهة/ألوهة when one is worshiped along with love, hope and desire. This is its meaning in the Arabic language. The meaning of الإلاهة is worship and the meaning is not lordship. Or the meaning is management of the affair. Due to this Ibn Abbas (رَضِيَ اللَّهُ عَنْهُمَا) would recite the verse as is reported from him by way of various routes of transmission indicating its authenticity of that which has been ascribed to him.[1] He would recite the statement of Allah in surah Al-A'raf: وَيَذَرَكَ وءالهتك

Meaning: Your worship; because he was worshiped, and he did not worship. He extracted this from the statement of Allah:

﴿مَا عَلِمْتُ لَكُم مِّنْ إِلَٰهٍ غَيْرِى﴾

"I have not known you to have a God other than Me." (Al-Qasas 28:38)

---

[1] Refer to Tafsir ibn Kathir (1/123)

Therefore, *Al-Ilahah* bears the meaning of worship. What indicates this is the statement of the poet within the well-known poem:

«لِلَّهِ دَرُّ الغانِياتِ المُدَّهِ... سَبَّحْنَ وَاسْتَرْجَعْنَ مِنْ تَأَلُّهِي»

"To Allah belongs all material richness...,
Glorified and Exalted is He above me of my worship."

Meaning, He is not in need of me worshiping Him. Hence, the term Allah, the listener understands from it the meaning of worship in truth for the one who deserves to be worshiped in truth. And the meaning of lordship does not occur to one's mind. Rather, the one who deserves to be deified in truth deserves to be worshiped to the exclusion of other than Him. And without doubt it comprises within it that He is the owner of lordship and that He deserves lordship because none deserves lordship exclusively except the One who within his hand is the dominion of everything. Due to this you find within the Qur'an oftentimes that Allah utilizes as evidence against the polytheist in their objection to the Tawheed of Allah's right to be worshiped alone their affirmation of the Tawheed of Allah's lordship and the details of this will come. Therefore, the statement of the person that says 'Bismillah' in this he is to bear in mind that these names belong to the true object of worship. Therefore, in doing so one removes from his heart every name of those false deities and the heart remains pure in its devotion towards Him and in the beginning of the recitation he does so for Allah, the Majestic and High, alone; to the exclusion of other than Him.

The Meaning of: "The Most Merciful, the Bestower of Mercy"

"The Most Merciful, the Bestower of Mercy," are two descriptions of the majestic phrase (Allah). Ar-Rahman is the first description and Ar-Rahim is the second description. And perhaps Ar-Rahim is the description of Ar-Rahman seeing how Ar-Rahman indicates the one who is described with mercy. Ar-Rahman and Ar-Rahim are two names from the names of Allah the Majestic and High. And they comprise the attribute of mercy for Allah the Majestic and High. And Ar-Rahman is more general and more exhaustive and further reaching than Ar-Rahim. Ar-Rahman indicates emphasis of mercy and it is the greatest form of emphasis, most vast and exhaustive and it is further reaching in terms of effect and connection than Ar-Rahim. Due to this some of the scholars have said that Ar-Rahman is the one who is merciful in the dunya as well as the hereafter and Ar-Rahim is the one who is merciful in the hereafter.[1] However, we

---

[1] Refer to Tafsir ibn Kathir (1/124). It is said that he is Ar-Rahman in the dunya as well as the hereafter and Ar-Rahim in the dunya as well as the hereafter. Al-Hakim reported within Al-Mustadrak in the

say that what is correct is that there is a difference between them.[1] And that Ar-Rahman is more general and exhausted than Ar-Rahim. Ar-Rahim is specific and it means the one who possesses a specific type of mercy. The specific mercy of Allah the Majestic and High is only for the believers. As for His general mercy, then it encompasses everything as Allah the Exalted has said:

﴿وَرَحْمَتِي وَسِعَتْ كُلَّ شَيْءٍ ۚ﴾

"My mercy encompasses all things." (Al-A'raf 7:156)

Hence, the mercy of Allah encompasses everything. Allah the Exalted has said:

﴿رَبَّنَا وَسِعْتَ كُلَّ شَيْءٍ رَّحْمَةً وَعِلْمًا﴾

"Our Lord, You have encompassed all things in mercy and knowledge." (Ghafir 40:7) [2]

---

book of *Supplications, The dua of the fulfillment of a debt* (1/514) (no. 1941) from the hadith of Aisha (رَضِيَ اللَّهُ عَنْهَا) on the authority of Abu Bakr from the prophet (صَلَّى اللَّهُ عَلَيْهِ وَسَلَّمَ) that he said:

«اللَّهُمَّ فَارِجَ الْهَمِّ، كَاشِفَ الْغَمِّ، مُجِيبَ دَعْوَةِ الْمُضطَرِّينَ، رَحْمنَ الدُّنْيَا وَالآخِرَةِ وَرَحِيمَهُمَا أَنْتَ تَرْحَمُنِي فَارْحَمْنِي بِرَحْمَةٍ تُغْنِينِي بِهَا عَنْ رَحْمَةِ مَنْ سِوَاكَ»

"O Allah the Remover of distress, the lifter of grief, the one who answers the supplication of those who are in difficulty, Rahman in the dunya and the hereafter and Rahim in them as well, have mercy upon me with the mercy and cover me with it that none can suffice in me mercy from anyone besides you."

[1] Refer to Tafsir At-Tabari (1/125). As well as Dur Al-Maslul (1/30) and Tafsir ibn Kathir (1/124).

[2] It is reported by Al-Bukhari within his sahih at the beginning of the book at the beginning of revelation (no. 3194) from the hadith of

Therefore, when the person says, In the name of Allah the Most Merciful, he is describing Allah the Majestic and High, praising Him by way of this name which contains the attribute of mercy that is a description containing the greatness effect and connection to His creation and it encompasses everything. Therefore, the servant is included in His general mercy and he needs along with that the specific mercy. Due to this Allah is likewise described with His statement: **"Ar-Rahim, the Bestower of Mercy."**

Without doubt this is from Allah the Majestic and High educating His servants and this is from mercy upon His servants that he begins his speech with this Bismillah that the servants are in need of and Allah the Majestic and High is not in need of that. However, He loves that His servant should praise Him. And He loves that His servant should extol Him and that his tongue should be busy as well as his actions with oprading and extolling Him, Glorified and Exalted be He.

✪✪✪

Abu Huraryah (رَضِيَ اللَّهُ عَنْهُ) who said: *"The messenger of Allah* (صَلَّى اللَّهُ عَلَيْهِ وَسَلَّمَ) *said:*

«إِنَّ اللَّه تَعَالَى لَمَّا قَضَى الْخَلْق كَتَبَ عِنْده فَوْق عَرْشه إِنَّ رَحْمَتِي غَلَبَتْ غَضَبِي»

"When Allah completed the creation He wrote within His book that is with Him above the throne, 'Indeed my mercy supersedes my wrath.'"

It was likewise reported by Muslim within his sahih in the book of *Tawbah Chapter: Reviving the Vastness of the Mercy of Allah the Exalted* and that it supersedes His Wrath (no.2751).

The Benefits of: "In the Name of Allah the Most Merciful, The bestower of Mercy"

We know from that which has preceded that when you utter this tremendous statement, "In the name of Allah the Most Merciful, The bestower of Mercy" in this verse then it opens your heart to various types of acts of worship for Allah the Majestic and High which you are not cognitive of without having knowledge of the meanings of the names of Allah the Majestic and High. And the subtlety of this is not affirmed with us. Hence, the statement: **"In the Name of Allah the Most Merciful, The bestower of Mercy,"** comes after the seeking of refuge and it places within the soul a type of fear, is this not the case? And the statement, **"In the name of Allah the Most Merciful, The bestower of Mercy"** contains opening within the soul the door of hope in Allah, the Majestic and High, and love for Allah and entrusting one's affair to Him; believing that Allah is the one who grants success and that He is the one who guides and that He is the one who blesses the servant when he reads in that which he recites and that which he eats and that which he drinks and in all affairs. Therefore, it opens the heart to two doors. The first door is the door of fear and the second door is the door of hope in Allah, the Majestic and High, as well as excellence in placing one's reliance upon Him and entrusting one's affair to Him, Glorified and Exalted be He.

The Meaning of: "All praise is for Allah, The Lord of All That Exists."

This is the first verse within Surah Al-Fatihah. It contains praise upon Allah by way of his *Hamd*. As has preceded within the hadith of Abu Hurayrah (رَضِيَٱللَّهُعَنْهُ) that was reported by Muslim in his sahih that when the servant says: **"All the praise is for Allah, the lord of all that exists,"** Allah the Majestic and High says: **"My servant has praised me."**[1]

✿✿✿

[1] Ibn Taymiyyah (رَحِمَهُٱللَّهُ) said with Majmu' Al-Fatawa(14/8): "This text affirms that this surah is divided between Allah and His servant and that these two statements are the division point within the surah wherein Allah said, **"You alone we worship..."**along with that which came before it is all for Allah and when He says, **"You alone we ask for help"** along with whatever came after it is for the servant. The servant shall have what he has asked for. Due to this one of the Salaf said, 'Half of it is praise and half of it is request and each of the two is from worship and seeking of assistance is dua.'"

The Meaning of Al-Hamd

Al-Hamd is praise along with love for the one that is praised. For if praise is devoid of love it is called Madh المدح and Allah the Majestic and High is mamduh ممدوح and mahmoud محمود (praised with love and praised due to Him being worthy of praise) and hamd of Him is greater than madh of Him, the Majestic and High be He. Because al-Madh can perhaps be devoid of love. As for al-Hamd this is praise due to Him having attributes of perfection and being worthy of praise and love. Due to this, the various types of praise shall come.

Therefore, when one says, "Praise is for Allah, the lord of all that exists" the meaning is all types of praise and every type of exaltation Allah the true object of worship is deserving of. He is the one who is the lord of all that exists. Meaning, the one who manages the creation in their various types, that which is upon land, that which is upon sea, that which is within the earth, that which is in the heavens, that which we know and that which we do not know, that which we see and that which we do not see, that which we hear and that which we do not hear. So all types of praise is for Allah the Majestic and High who possesses complete lordship over His creation all together is deserving of that. And the phrase

Al-Hamd is comprised of two parts. The Arabic definite article ا and ل along with hamd and concerning the Arabic definite article ا and ل the scholars have said regarding it[1], that it is placed here to denote all types of something. The meaning of that is that when you say Al-Hamd this means all types and categories of praise is for Allah, the lord of all that exists.

So What Are the Types and Categories That Allah is Deserving of?

The types are many. However, that which brings them together are five and if the servant bears them in mind or if he bears one of them in mind every time he recites the statement of Allah: **"All the praise is for Allah, the lord of all that exists"** then, all types of love shall be opened for him. As well as His glorification and awe and excellent manners of praise for Allah shall occur to him. As well as different types of knowledge and heart based worship that none knows except the one who is aware of them and enacts them, shall be facilitated for him. They are as follows:

✪✪✪

[1] Refer to Tafsir At-Tabari (1/138) and Dur Al-Masun (1/37). Tafsir ibn Kathir (1/131)

The Various Types of Praises Are for Allah the Majestic and High

Indeed the types of praise that are for Allah, the Majestic and High, are five:

The First Type: He, the Glorified and High, is worthy of praise for He is one in His Lordship and He is the Lord, the Owner, the Master, the Controller within this universe in its entirety. There is no lord for this universe in its entirety other than Allah the Majestic and High. Hence, praises are showered upon Allah due to this description which is the fact that the Majestic and High be He, is the lord of the entirety of this universe and that He is the lord of all that exists, the lord of all of its types and categories. Allah the Majestic and High be he said:

﴿الْحَمْدُ لِلَّهِ الَّذِى لَمْ يَتَّخِذْ وَلَدًا﴾

And say, "Praise to Allah, who has not taken a son."
(Al-Isra 17:111)

Likewise, Allah has said:

﴿ الْحَمْدُ لِلَّهِ فَاطِرِ السَّمَاوَاتِ وَالْأَرْضِ جَاعِلِ الْمَلَائِكَةِ رُسُلًا﴾

> **"[All] praise is [due] to Allah, the Creator of the heavens and the earth, [who] made the angels messengers"** (Fatir 35:1)

All of this is from the praises of Allah due to the meanings of lordship. One must bear the meanings of lordship in mind as well as their effects in the creation and call to mind the meaning of his lordship and its various types from management, distribution of goodness, withholding evil and His kindness and gentleness to His servants and His mercy upon them. Likewise, you must call to mind the effects of Allah's lordship upon the creation and due to all of that He is deserving of the greatest forms of praises in the most complete manner.

The Second Type: Allah the Majestic and High is worthy of praise because He deserves to be worshiped alone to the exclusion to anyone other than Him. Meaning, He alone is worthy of praise due to His divinity. So Allah, the Majestic and High, is the true and evident ilah. That which is besides Him from deities that are worshiped, the worship of them is done in transgression, oppression and excess. Therefore, He deserves that His servants worship Him and that they devote themselves to Him and that they love Him and that they hope in Him and that they fear Him and that they have good thoughts about Him and place their trust in Him and seek help from Him and seek refuge with Him, and seek salvation from Him. And that they slaughter for Him and that they pray to Him. All of that is for Him alone. Hence, Allah is praised because He alone deserves these affairs from His servants in their entirety of the various types and categories from that which is upon land, from that which is upon sea, from that which is within the sky. All of them glorify Allah and praise Him and worship Him alone without associating partners with Him. As for mankind, then those who worship Him alone not associating partners with Him are many.

The Third Type: Allah, the Majestic and High, is worthy of praise for He is the possessor of beautiful names and lofty attributes. Meaning, that He is praised because He has beautiful names which are the epitome of beauty and He is praiseworthy because He has lofty attributes; attributes of perfection, for He has the most perfect of attributes and He has from every attribute of perfection the most complete and perfect of that. He has no deficiencies whatsoever and evil is not attributed to Him. Rather, He is perfect in His names and attributes. His names and attributes have tremendous effects within the creation. The heart praises Him due to them with various types of praise. If one reflects and ponders upon an attribute of Allah or the name of Allah Al-Ghaffar (The All-Forgiving) he will see the effects of the forgiveness of Allah upon His servants. If one reflects upon the name of Allah Ar-Rahim (The Bestower of Mercy) he will see the effects of the mercy of Allah, the Majestic and High, which He distributes between His servants. If you look at the name of Allah Al-Aziz (The All Mighty) you will see the might of Allah the Majestic and High and how He has made the honor to be for Him and for His book, for His messengers and the believers. When you look at the names of Allah, the Majestic and High, you see that each name has its effect within this life and it has an effect within the universe of Allah, the Majestic and High, without doubt.

So if the servant contemplates upon this and knows the meaning of the names and attributes of Allah, the Majestic and High, he will be filled with praises upon Allah out of love, the praises which consists of Al-Hamd by way of something which one who is ignorant of Allah is incapable of praising Him with. Due to this, the most beloved speech to Allah the Majestic and High is when one declares Him to be free of any imperfections and affirming His attributes of perfection. As has come at the end of the hadith that is in Sahih Al-Bukhari[1] in which it is mentioned that the Prophet (صَلَّى اللَّهُ عَلَيْهِ وَسَلَّمَ) said:

«كَلِمَتَانِ خَفِيفَتَانِ عَلَى اللِّسَانِ، ثَقِيلَتَانِ فِي الْمِيزَانِ، حَبِيبَتَانِ إِلَى الرَّحْمَنِ: (سُبْحَانَ اللَّهِ وَبِحَمْدِهِ)، (سُبْحانَ اللَّهِ الْعَظِيمِ) »

"There are two words which are beloved to Ar-Rahman, light upon the tongue, heavy upon the scales they are, 'SubhanAllahi wa bi-hamdihi (Free is Allah of imperfections and the praise be to Him), and SubhanAllahil Adheem (Free is Allah of imperfections and He is Magnificent)."

This supplication contains within it At-Tasbih (declaring that Allah is free of imperfections) as well as Al-Hamd (praising Allah) and they are from the greatest of speech in this regard.

The Fourth Type: is that Allah the Mighty and Majestic is praised for sending down his magnificent book. As Allah has said:

---

[1] In the book of Tawheed (no.7563). Refer to as well (no.6406 and 6682 and 7563) from the hadith of Abu Hurayrah (رَضِيَ اللَّهُ عَنْهُ). See as well Fath Al-Bari (13/540).

﴿الْحَمْدُ لِلَّهِ الَّذِي أَنزَلَ عَلَىٰ عَبْدِهِ الْكِتَابَ وَلَمْ يَجْعَل لَّهُ عِوَجًا ۜ ١﴾

"[All] praise is [due] to Allah, who has sent down upon His Servant the Book and has not made therein any deviance." (Kahf 18:1)

Hence, He is praised for every command that is within the Qur'an and every prohibition. He is praiseworthy and lauded on the account of that because the commands of Allah, the Majestic and High, contain within them His love. Meaning, He loves them and He loves for His servants to avoid His prohibitions. Hence, His commands and His prohibitions are beloved to Him; when one adheres to His commands and avoids His prohibitions. Therefore, praises are showered upon Allah, the Majestic and High due to Him sending down the book for the guidance of mankind by way of these commands which bring about the rectification of mankind and all of that which He has legislated. Whether, that be within the rulings of worship or in the rulings of social interactions or whether that be in that which is specific to an individual or that which is specific to a community or that which is in relation to action based rulings or that which is in relation to information; meaning, in the affairs of creed. Allah is praised for all of this and he who knows these meanings when he recites the statement of Allah:

﴿الْحَمْدُ لِلَّهِ الَّذِي أَنزَلَ عَلَىٰ عَبْدِهِ الْكِتَابَ وَلَمْ يَجْعَل لَّهُ عِوَجًا ۜ ١﴾

"[All] praise is [due] to Allah, who has sent down upon His Servant the Book and has not made therein any deviance." (Kahf 18:1)

He would know the meaning of the praises that are being showered upon Allah due to Him sending down the book and that He, the Majestic and High be He, is praised for this tremendous blessing upon His servant.

The Fifth, (and final type): Allah, the Majestic and High, is praiseworthy; meaning, praises are showered upon Him due to that which He has commanded within the universe and that which He has decreed within the universe and that which He has preordained for His servants. What enters into this are the blessings that He has bestowed upon them because they are from that which He has made to be a blessing connected to His commands and the affairs within the universe. This is that which all are aware of or many amongst mankind are aware of when one says: "*The praise is for Allah...,*" one bears in mind the meanings of praising Allah for these blessings. And this is just one among many types and one category amongst various categories of praises for Allah, the Majestic and High.

Therefore, the types of praises for Allah the Majestic and High are many and cannot be enumerated. The heart of the believer is incapable of bearing all of them. So, it is befitting that the believer accustoms himself to contemplation upon one of the types of praises with which he praises Allah, the Majestic and High, within his prayer. Praising Him, the Majestic and High, at the end of the prayer and that he bears in mind one of these types, contemplating upon it. (Saying) *The praise is for Allah, the praise is for Allah, the praise is for Allah.* Meaning, when one says the adhkar after the completion of the prayer he bears in mind these meanings and he thinks about, for example, that He the Majestic and High is praiseworthy for His Lordship and the effect of the Lordship within the creation and the meanings of that Lordship; then within the next prayer he praises Allah with the second type and so on until he accustoms himself and his heart to praising Allah, the Majestic and High, with the various types of praise. Due to this there has come within the long and well-known hadith of the intercession that the Prophet (صَلَّىٱللَّهُعَلَيْهِوَسَلَّمَ) said:

«فَأَنْطَلِقُ فَآتِي تَحْتَ الْعَرْشِ، فَأَقَعُ سَاجِدًا لِرَبِّي عَزَّ وَجَلَّ ثُمَّ يَفْتَحُ اللَّهُ عَلَيَّ مِنْ مَحَامِدِهِ وَحُسْنِ الثَّنَاءِ عَلَيْهِ شَيْئًا لَمْ يَفْتَحْهُ عَلَى أَحَدٍ قَبْلِي»

"I will proceed forth and come; then I will fall down prostrate beneath the throne, prostrating before my lord and Allah will reveal to me words of praise and excellent statements of exaltation which He had not revealed to anyone before me..."[1]

Contemplate upon his statement: **"Then Allah will reveal to me statements of praise and excellent statements of exaltation which He had not revealed to anyone before me."**

He, upon be him be prayers and peace is the most knowledge of the creation regarding his lord and the best of

[1] Reported by Al-Bukhari within his sahih in the book of Tafsir, chapter: *The Statement of Allah, 'The Progeny of Those Whom We Carried Along With Nuh, Indeed He Was A Thankful Slave'* (no.4712) from the hadith of Abu Hurayrah (رَضِيَٱللَّهُعَنْهُ). Muslim likewise reported it within his sahih in the book of Iman, chapter: *The Lowest of the People of Paradise in Station* (no.193) with the wording, *"And I shall praise my lord the Exalted with praises that my lord would teach me then I would intercede."* from the hadith of Anas (رَضِيَٱللَّهُعَنْهُ) see as well (no.194).

them in praising Him and the most eloquent of them in describing Him and showering praises upon Him, in spite of this Allah will reveal to him types of praises for Allah because the praise of Allah the Majestic and High is such that none who praise him are able to fully encompass that no matter what they may have been given. Without doubt this is from that which softens the heart of the believer out of awe of Allah and praise of Allah and love and veneration of Him. Then it is said, "Allah the Majestic and High would say, 'O Muhammad raise your head ask and you shall be given intercede and your intercession shall be accepted...'" When a person says:

﴿الْحَمْدُ لِلَّهِ رَبِّ الْعَالَمِينَ ۝٢﴾

"All praises be to Allāh, the Lord of all that exists."
(Fatihah 1:2)

These are the five types of praise. All of the types of praise and each category of praise is for Allah.

✿✿✿

The Meaning of: 'Lilllah' (For Allah)

Its meaning is that Allah is deserving of them and the ل within the statement, لِلَّهِ 'Lilllah' is referred to as the ل of actualization. The meaning of actualization here is ownership. Therefore, Allah is the owner of praises. Likewise, He is the one who deserves them the Majestic and High be He. No one deserves them in this manner except Him, Glorified and Exalted be He. As for the creation perhaps one may deserve a specific type amongst these types of praise. However, in the greatest manner none deserves it except Allah alone. If in most cases the words come before the ل then it is referred to as the ل of ownership and if it comes before the words then it is known as the ل of actualization. For example, one says, الكتاب لفلان (the book belongs to such and such)" this is the ل of ownership because that which is in front of it is identified but if that which is before it is specific it becomes the ل of actualization. As is said, "الفخر لفلان (bragging rights belong to such and such). And, "الكبرياء لله (greatness belongs to Allah)." Therefore the phrase, *Al-hamdulillah* means Allah is deserving of praise.

The Meaning of: "The Lord of All that Exists"

you notice here that there is a distinction between lordship and divinity, the true object of worship is being described as being the lord of all that exists. This is the greatest evidence that lordship is not divinity and lordship has a specific meaning and that divinity has a specific meaning. This is that which the Arabic language necessitates.

The Meaning of Rabb in the Arabic Language

Rabb in the Arabic language is the one who controls the universe and manages its dominion. He is the master, the one who is obeyed in His commands, with the lordship of Allah the Majestic and High over the Alamin is clear. It is that He is the one that controls this universe and manages it and He is the one who administers His command and no one can amend His judgements. No one can repel His decree. No one can follow up His command within His universe. Due to this, we know the mistake of the people of innovation from the Asha'irah and their likes who explain Uluhiyah to be Rububiyah. As the people of theological rhetoric say: Al-Ilah is the one who has the capability of inventing and Allah is the proper name for the one who has the capability of inventing. The ability to invent is from the meanings of lordship and it is not from the meanings of divinity, neither in the Arabic language nor within the specific custom of the Arabs. Due to this, Al-Sanusi said within his aqeedah known as Umm Al-Baraheen: "We declare Allah distant from them and from their innovations, statements, oppositions and deviation in the explanation of Al-Ilah. For Al-Ilah is the one who is not in need of anyone else while everyone is in need of Him." He went on to say: "Therefore, the meaning of la ilaha ill'Allah is: No one is free of need of everyone and no one is exempt of need of Him other than Allah."

The meaning of this is that he explains lordship to be divinity. This verse is a refutation against them and the explanation of divinity to be lordship is the greatest of that which will lead to the notion that those who associate partners in worship with Him are not disbelievers because they do not reject lordship, for they affirm that Allah is the one that has the capability of originating and He is the one who is free of need for any besides Himself. And He is such that all besides Him are in need of Him. So, how then will they be disbelievers? Explaining Uluhiyyah to be worship negates this principle at its foundation. Due to this, within this verse is a clear evidence for the distinction between lordship and divinity.

The meaning of Al-Alamin (all that exists)

The lord of all that exists, the Lord is the description for the majestic term (i.e. Allah) and Al-Alamin is the plural of Al-Alam and Al-Alam likewise is plural. It is not singular in its meaning. Al-Alam is a genus under which there are various types; as has been mentioned by Shaykh Muhammad ibn Abdul Wahhab (رَحِمَهُ ٱللَّهُ) within the *Three Fundamental Principles*, wherein he said, "Everything besides Allah is Alam and I am a part of that Alam." And the Awalim (Various types of alam) are many. There is the world of the jinn, there is the world of humanity, the world of the angels, the bird world, the animal world, the plant world, that of wind; they are all various types all being referred to as Alam because by way of them it is known that he who has brought them into existence by way of complete and perfect lordship is deserving of worship and truth. Therefore, the Lord of the Alamin means all of these various types of Al-Alam of that which you know and that which you do not know. For everything other than Allah is Alam and you are a part of the Alam.

Hence, everything besides Allah which is beneath the throne and other than it enters into the lordship of Allah the Majestic and High, this is the meaning of this verse wherein one says all the praise is for Allah the lord of all that exists. Therefore, its meaning with this detail comes to be: all types of praise in every category of laudation, Allah is deserving of it. He is the true object of worship. The one who manages and controls the creation. The one whose commands are authoritative within all realms and this is in reference to everything besides Allah. Without doubt this will open the heart to all of these affairs.

Note: Some of the scholars have stated that the meaning of رَبِّ الْعَالَمِينَ *The **Lord of All that Exists*** is: the One that cultivates, and Allah is the one who has nurtured all of the creation by way of His blessings. He has nurtured the entirety of the universe by bringing them into existence gradually. The origin of Rabb, as I have mentioned, shares the same origin as At-Tarbiyyah and this is gradualness in caregiving. It is said رباه meaning he has nurtured him, i.e. He gradually took care of him in a manner that was befitting for him. The lord is the one who is the master, the one that is obeyed, the one who manages and controls. The One who is over other than himself or gradually takes care of him with that which is beneficial for him. This is due to his need for that. As for Allah the Majestic and High be he is not in need of anyone. Rather, all of the creation are in need of Him in all of their affairs. And if anyone were to be without Allah for the twinkling of an eye they would have been destroyed.[1] I ask Allah, the Majestic and High, to make us from the Alamin, mentioned within his book.

✡✡✡

---

[1] Allah has said within the Qur'an:

﴿يَا أَيُّهَا النَّاسُ أَنتُمُ الْفُقَرَاءُ إِلَى اللَّهِ ۖ وَاللَّهُ هُوَ الْغَنِيُّ الْحَمِيدُ ﴿١٥﴾ إِن يَشَأْ
يُذْهِبْكُمْ وَيَأْتِ بِخَلْقٍ جَدِيدٍ ﴿١٦﴾ وَمَا ذَٰلِكَ عَلَى اللَّهِ بِعَزِيزٍ ﴿١٧﴾﴾

"O mankind, you are those in need of Allah, while Allah is the Free of need, the Praiseworthy. If He wills, He can do away with you and bring forth a new creation. And that is for Allah not difficult." (Al-Fatir 35:15-17)

Wisdoms Derived from the Person Reciting the Isti'adhah (Seeking of Refuge) and the Basmalah Along with the Statement, All the Praise is for Allah Lord of All That Exists

The scholars have said regarding this verse it opens the door of love for Allah, the Majestic and High. Know that the seeking of refuge opens the door of fear and the Basmalah opens the door of hope. Whereas the statement:

﴿الْحَمْدُ لِلَّهِ﴾

"All praises be to Allāh"

opens the door of love for Allah, the Majestic and High; the One to whom is this description is to be loved and the One who is described how he is described deserves praise; and He is the Lord of all that exists and He is the one who owns the entirety of this universe and He is the one whom in His hand is all things. He distributes goodness to whomever He wills and He withholds it from whomever He wills. He bestows glory upon whomever He wills, He humiliates whomever He wills. This is the powerful, the All-Mighty. This is the one who possesses these attributes and these descriptions and His majesty. Does not He deserve to be loved? Without doubt, He deserves to be loved. The verse which comes after it is the statement of Allah:

﴿الرَّحْمَٰنِ الرَّحِيمِ ۝٣﴾

"The Most-Merciful, the Bestower of Mercy."
(Al-Fatihah 1:3)

This likewise opens the door of hope. Note that hope is returned to again. Then, within His statement:

﴿مَالِكِ يَوْمِ الدِّينِ ۝٤﴾

"Owner of the Day of Recompense." (Al-Fatihah 1:4)

This opens the door of fear; which is a reference for the day of recompense. So, fear is returned to again. Hence, when the person recites beginning with: *"I seek refuge with Allah from the accursed Shaytan, in the Name of Allah the Most Merciful, the Bestower of Mercy, all the praise is for Allah the lord of all that exists,"* He transitions from fear to hope to love. Then, he transitions from love with his statement: **"All the praise is for Allah the lord of all that exists,"** to hope with his statement: **"The Most Merciful the Bestower of Mercy,"** then back to fear with his statement: **"Owner of the Day of Recompense."** Then, there shall come details regarding his statement: **"You alone we worship..."** We shall mention this explanation in detail in'sha-Allah.

This means that worship is built upon these three pillars: love, fear, and hope; since your love for Allah makes you move for the sake of Allah. And the love for the people of dunya makes you move for the sake of the dunya. The love of those who love kings makes them move for the sake of their kings and so on. So the love of the believer makes him move in obedience to Allah. However, this movement can perhaps stop. Therefore, it is a must that one have hope in the mercy of Allah, the Majestic and High, and his hope for Allah, the Majestic and High, will not stop as long as he is living. Due to this, one begins with the Basmalah which contains mention of mercy and in that is hope as one says: *"The Most Merciful, the Bestower of Mercy."* After that comes the statement: *"All the praise is for Allah the Lord of all that exists, the Most Merciful, the Bestower of Mercy,"* which likewise contains hope. Hence, the first thing that one says is the seeking of refuge and this ends with the statement, "Owner of the Day of Recompense." and this denotes fear. This is since the one who loves Allah, the Majestic and High, has hope in Him and moves in pursuit of His pleasure. He is not perpetually firm upon this path, neither looking towards the right nor to the left; and he does not take any path except in a state of fear. Thus, these verses come together giving life to the heart with the greatest forms of Al-Iman, which are the pillars of worship upon which worship is predicated in the most complete manner. Thus, by way of it true worship is established in the most complete fashion.

✿✿✿

The Meaning of: "The Most Merciful, the Bestower of Mercy"

The statement of Allah the Majestic and High:

﴿الرَّحْمَٰنِ الرَّحِيمِ﴾

"The Most Merciful, the Bestower of Mercy"

Contains two names amongst the beautiful Names of Allah. They are, within this place linguistically, two descriptions of the name Allah. Hence, they are two descriptions of the majestic term. They are descriptions for the entity indicated by the majestic term, Allah. So, the statement: **'The Lord of all that exists'** is the first description and **Ar-Rahman** is the second description and **Ar-Rahim** is the third description. **Owner of the Day of Recompense** is the fourth description. The verse: **"The Most Merciful, the Bestower of Mercy,"** contains two names from the beautiful names of Allah that embodies the attribute of mercy for Allah, the Majestic and High. Hence, the name of Allah, Ar-Rahman encompassing the attribute of mercy is broader, greater and further reaching in its connection than the name of Allah Ar-Rahim, in encompassing the attribute of mercy. We have already mentioned that Ar-Rahman is the one who is described with vast mercy, that covers all times; in the dunya as well as the hereafter and mercy is from the attributes of Allah's self. Whereas Ar-Rahim encompasses the attribute of mercy in the hereafter. And this is that which the Tafsir of the Salaf indicates. As has been mentioned by Ibn Kathir (رَحِمَهُ ٱللَّهُ) that Ar-Rahman is Rahman in the dunya as well as the hereafter. Whereas, Ar-Rahim is Rahim in the hereafter. Allah, the Majestic and High, is described as being the possessor of mercy. Allah, the Majestic and High, has said:

﴿وَرَحْمَتِي وَسِعَتْ كُلَّ شَيْءٍ ۚ﴾

"My mercy encompasses all things." (Al-A'raf 7:156)

Therefore, His mercy encompasses everything and the term shay' شيء is a noun for that which is known. His mercy the Majestic and High encompasses every known thing and it is known that His statement, "All that exists," as that which has preceded from our speech indicates that it is the plural of alam. And Al-Alam indicates all types of Awalim; because it is known that Allah the Majestic and High is the Creator who is singled out in creation. He is singled out in creation, provision, giving life, causing death and all of the meanings of lordship. Hence, this is why it is appropriate to mention the name of Allah, Ar-Rahman after mentioning: **"...The Lord of all that exists,"** because this includes the attribute of mercy which is connected to everything either in the dunya or in the Hereafter. As for within the dunya then the connection of Allah's mercy is to everything. As Allah has said, **"And my mercy encompasses everything."** The mercy of Allah the Majestic and High is evident in that it encompasses the throne and that which is around it, the footstool and that which is beneath it. And the heavens are established by way of the mercy of Allah, the Majestic and High, within the heavens. Hence, the heavens are not independent nor is which is within them nor that which is between them from the mercy of Allah, the Majestic and High, even for a twinkling of an eye. Allah says:

﴿إِنَّ اللَّهَ يُمْسِكُ السَّمَاوَاتِ وَالْأَرْضَ أَن تَزُولَا ۚ وَلَئِن زَالَتَا إِنْ أَمْسَكَهُمَا مِنْ أَحَدٍ مِّن بَعْدِهِ ۚ إِنَّهُ كَانَ حَلِيمًا غَفُورًا ﴿٤١﴾﴾

"Indeed, Allah holds the heavens and the earth, lest they cease. And if they should cease, no one could hold them [in place] after Him. Indeed, He is Forbearing and Forgiving." (Fatir 35:41)

Meaning, that which is within the heavens or this dunya from the various types of creations nor the various types of that which fly within the sky nor that which is within it from the various types of that which Allah has created from that which we know from air and its like, and from that which we do not know; all of that is from the mercy of Allah, the Majestic and High, upon the creation itself. And from the mercy of Allah the Majestic and High upon those who benefit from those created things. When you look at the Earth and its various types of mountains, valleys, that which is hard, that which is soft, its trees, etc., you will see that all of them stand by the mercy of Allah, the Majestic and High. All of that is proven by way of this name, **"Ar-Rahman."** Due to this, Allah has stated: **"The Lord of all that exists, the Most Merciful...,"** because His mercy is connected to all that exists. When you look at the ocean and you look at that which is in the ocean itself and at the various types of that which is within the Earth and that which is beneath the Earth from living creatures and that which is within it from the various types of creation of Allah, the Majestic and High, the living and that which is not living you will attain certainty that all of that only lives by the mercy of Allah the Majestic and High. And this has a strong effect upon the heart of the servant in knowing the effects of the mercy of Allah and the effects of the name of Allah, Ar-Rahman in proportion with that. Ibn Jarir (رَحِمَهُ ٱللَّهُ) reported within his Tafsir that there is agreement regarding the connection of the mercy that is in the name of Allah, Ar-Rahman to the dunya as well as the hereafter. As for the name of Allah, Ar-Rahim then it is connected to the hereafter.[1] Due to this, we say the encompassing of the mercy of Allah the Majestic and High of the disbelievers is a spoil for them in the dunya for they enter into the connection of mercy within the name of Allah, Ar-Rahman. For the disbeliever, receives mercy in this dunya of various types. Allah the Majestic and High said:

﴿وَمَن كَفَرَ فَأُمَتِّعُهُ قَلِيلًا﴾

"And whoever disbelieves - I will grant him enjoyment for a little;" (Al-Baqarah 2:126)

The disbeliever enjoys various types of pleasure within the dunya and he lives a life that perhaps is considered to be a stable and good life while he is a disbeliever committing shirk with Allah and disbelief in Allah and the refuge is with Allah. However, the mercy of Allah the Majestic and High is general within this dunya encompassing everything. As for

[1] Refer to Tafsir ibn Jarir (1/126).

in the hereafter in the name of Allah, Ar-Rahim is specific to the believers in the hereafter. Allah the Majestic and High said:

﴿وَكَانَ بِالْمُؤْمِنِينَ رَحِيمًا ۝٤٣﴾

"And ever is He, to the believers, Merciful."
(Al-Ahzab 33:43)

Hence, mercy is repeated and mentioned for the believers in the hereafter with the name of Allah, Ar-Rahman and with the name of Allah, Ar-Rahim and the mercy is repeated and mentioned for the believers in the dunya with a specific mercy for them as Allah has said:

"The Lord of all that exists" and then thereafter said: **"Ar-Rahman."** Due to this the people of knowledge say that these two names Ar-Rahman and Ar-Rahim opens the vastest of doors for those who comprehend them for the love of Allah the Majestic and High and they are open for the one who understands them the vastest of doors for the hope in Allah. Allah, the Majestic and High, has said within the hadith Qudsi:

«أَنَا عِنْدَ ظَنِّ عَبْدِي بِي، فَلْيَظُنَّ بِي مَا شَاءَ»

"I am as my servant thinks that I am so therefore, let him think regarding me that which he wishes."[1]

I have mentioned in that which has preceded that the statement of Allah, **"The Lord of all that exists,"** opens the door of love and that the statement here, **"The Most**

[1] Reported by Ahmad within his Musnad (25/394) (no.16,016). As well as (28/187) (no.16,979) from the hadith of Wathilah ibn Al-Asqa'.

Merciful, the Bestower of Mercy" opens the door of hope within the heart.

The field of the names and attributes of Allah have been delved into by many of the scholars of tafsir in this place. That which we will mention from it is the mercy of Allah the Majestic and High, repeating its affirmation. This is that the mercy of Allah is something which is with Allah, the Majestic and High. Mercy is an attribute that is Dhatiyah (connected to His being). Thus, it is with Allah the Majestic and High. The mercy of Allah and that which is similar to it from attributes, perhaps are difficult to explain with a meaning that encompasses each and every aspect of it. This is because all-inclusive meanings are not something which are present in its entirety except within the minds. As for in reality, and in that which is in existence outside of the minds one description is present in attachment of certain things to other things. So it is said: "The mercy of one person to another," or: "The mercy of the father to his child," or: "The mercy of a mother to her child." or: "The mercy of Allah to His creation" and the likes of this. Due to that, that which is from all-inclusive meanings is difficult to explain with an explanation that is suitable for that which is connected to the creation and that which is connected to the creator. Due to this, many of the scholars when they mention the explanation of rahmah or its like from those terms which are from the attributes of Allah the Majestic and High then they say, "Ar-Rahmah is an attribute." And they do not delve into its explanation. This is the meaning of the statement of the Salaf: *"Leave them as they have come."*[1] Because explaining them is such that perhaps the explainer will find that which is in it in connection to mercy and perhaps he will find within it that which is connected to the creation. Due to this, many of the people of innovation have gone astray. For they have explained mercy with the mercy that is between the creation and they have said: "Mercy is understood as the inclination of the heart to the one that displays mercy." And this explanation is how mercy is in relation to the human being. And this is from the great errors in the explanation of these terms. Hence, the attributes which are not entities that can be restricted, are terms. Because they have explained it with some of that which is connected to it; and it is the creation. And due to that which they thought about in relation to it they said: "Therefore, it is not suitable as an attribute for Allah." And they did not explain mercy from the viewpoint of an all-inclusive general meaning which is suitable for all that which is described with it. They only explained it with some of that which it can be described with and that is the creation, then, they hastened to negate it from the one who has been described with it, and this is the Creator, Glorified be He. Due to this they distort its meaning and they say that mercy is wanting goodness for someone else. And they, I am

---

[1] Shaykh Al-Islam Ibn Taymiyyah he mentioned within Majmu' Al-Fatawa (5/39), "Abu Bakr Al-Khalal narrated within Kitab As-Sunnah on the authority of Al-Waleed ibn Muslim that he said, "I asked Malik ibn Anas, Sufyan At-Thawri, Al-Layth ibn Sa'd, and Al-Awza'i regarding reports that have come mentioning the attributes and they said: 'Leave them as they have come.' (In another narration they said, 'Leave them as they have come without delving into the howness.)'"

referring to Asha'irah, the Maturidiyah, the Kulabiyah and those similar to them—explained it with this explanation because *wanting,* according to them, is an attribute that indicates intellect and they (only) affirm seven attributes for Allah. Each attribute within the Qur'an that is not from the seven attributes which they affirm by way of what the intellect can conceive, they return the explanation in the Qur'an to one of the seven aforementioned attributes due to that which their intellects can grasp. So they say that mercy is wanting goodness. Whereas, anger is wanting vengeance. Pleasure is wanting to bestow blessings and the likes of that. So they explain these attributes by way of Al-Iradah bil-Iradah (which) is one of the seven attributes which they affirm and this is their path as it relates to this verse and whatever resembles that. They say that it is a metaphor for goodness or wanting goodness.

Here we draw attention to something which is appropriate to be mentioned and it is that metaphoric usage of the attributes is falsehood. And this is because the people of metaphoric usage define metaphor as transitioning a term from its original place to another place due to there being an appropriate reason to do so and they place a condition that the first place of the term is known. Due to this, they transition this term from its first place to a second place due to there being an appropriate reason to do so (according to them). And it is falsehood that the first place is in description of Allah the Majestic and High of mercy that is known for transferring this term to the creation in the most complete manner and what is known from this is that which a portion of that meaning indicates. As for the mercy in its most complete meaning, which is the description of

Allah, this is not known. Due to that, it is not possible that the first place be something which is known. For this reason, the claim of all of Allah's attributes being metaphorical is falsehood because the first place based upon their definition is not something which is known. Thus, it is not possible to transfer it from an unknown place, as is the statement of the verifiers of the Arabic language and the scholars of tafsir and the various groups and scholars; and this is a point of benefit as it relates to this tremendous issue.[1]

✡✡✡

[1] Refer to Majmu' Al-Fatawa (20/443, 452, 455, and 458).

The Meaning of: "Owner of the Day of Recompense"

Allah, the Glorified and High, then says:

﴿مَالِكِ يَوْمِ الدِّينِ ۝٤﴾

"Owner of the Day of Recompense."
(Al-Fatihah 1:4)

This is a description after the previous descriptions. Thus, Al-Malik is from the names of Allah, the Majestic and High, for He is the master glorified be He. Therefore, here Allah refers to himself with 5 names. The first of them is that He is:

﴿الْحَمْدُ لِلَّهِ رَبِّ الْعَالَمِينَ ۝٢﴾

"All praises be to Allah, the Lord of all that exists."
(Al-Fatihah 1:2)

The Second: He is Ar-Rabb i.e., the **Lord** or the **Lord of all that exists.**

The Third: He is Ar-Rahman (the Most Merciful).

The Fourth: is that He is Ar-Rahim (the Bestower of Mercy).

The Fifth: He is the Owner of the Day of Judgment.

When you reflect upon these five names you find them to be such that all of the names emanate from them in terms of meaning. I have mentioned to you that the names of Allah the Majestic and High are such that from there are those that return to the meaning of majesty and from them are those that return to the meaning of beauty. From them are those who return to the meaning of lordship and from them are those who return to the meaning of divinity. Lordship is mentioned within the statement of Allah that He is: **"The Lord of all that exists."** And I have mentioned that with the statement that He is, "The **Master of the Day of Judgement"** this is a description of Majesty and I have mentioned the statement that He is, **"The Owner of the Day of Judgement,"** because this is what majesty brings about. As well as fear, trepidation, and awe of Him.

Similarly, descriptions of beauty are within the statement of Allah, **"The Most Merciful, the Bestower of Mercy."** Likewise, the attributes that return to divinity are within mention of His name, Allah which is the greatest of His names.

✿✿✿

Surah Al-Fatihah contains principles regarding the beautiful names of Allah.

Thus, within this chapter are principles connected to Allah's beautiful names as Ibn Al-Qayyim (رَحِمَهُ ٱللَّهُ) has mentioned as well as his shaykh, Shaykh Al-Islam Ibn Taymiyyah (رَحِمَهُ ٱللَّهُ) Many of the verifiers, may Allah have mercy upon them, have compiled issues related to the names and attributes of Allah.[1] So here he said: **"The Owner of the Day of Recompense,"** First, in terms of description of Allah, the Majestic and High, it brings about fear because the Day of Recompense is the day of reckoning and the day of calling to account.

---

[1] Refer to Madarij Al-Salikin (1/82 and 89).

The Wisdoms Behind the Person Reciting, "The Master of the Day of Recompense"

So the statement:

﴿مَالِكِ يَوْمِ الدِّينِ ﴿٤﴾﴾

"The Owner of the Day of Recompense."
(Al-Fatihah 1:4)

Brings about fear for the one who comprehends it. He who says it thinking about what is in his heart from the various types of doubts and desires which prevent him from consistently being obedient to his lord and he comprehends what he says, this will bring about fear of that day whereupon Allah will call the creation to account. Due to this, the scholars have stated that Allah begins within this chapter by mentioning that which will invoke within the servant love for Allah; and that is the Lordship of Allah, the Majestic and High, over all that exists. And they mention that which will invoke hope within the heart where He says:

"The Master of the Day of Recompense." There then is to come with mention of the statement:

﴿إِيَّاكَ نَعْبُدُ وَإِيَّاكَ نَسْتَعِينُ﴾

> **"It is You alone (O Allāh) that we worship and it is You alone that we ask for help (in Your obedience and in all of our affairs)."** (Al-Fatihah)

The reason for mentioning these three things together within these successive verses. Allah (سُبْحَانَهُ وَتَعَالَىٰ) said here, ﴿مَالِكِ يَوْمِ الدِّينِ﴾(The Owner of the Day of Recompense) it is also recited ﴿مَلِكِ يَوْمِ الدِّينِ﴾(The King of the Day of Judgement).[1]

Maalik is from the beautiful names of Allah and Malik is likewise from the beautiful names of Allah but there is a difference between them. Maalik is from *al-mulk* or *al-milk* and it refers to ownership of things. Just as you're saying: "I own a house." Or, "I own the book." As for Malik, then it is from al-mulk and the meaning of *al-mulk* is leadership, management and control. Perhaps a king or one who has sovereignty is not an owner of individual objects or kingdom. However, in that which he does own, his authority is administered and he manages and controls it. Allah the Majestic and High is described with both attributes and He is referred to by both names. This is the most comprehensive affair. Thus, when the heart of a human is attached to that which he sees within the kings of this

[1] Asim as well as Al-Kasa'i both recited it ﴿مَالِكِ يَوْمِ الدِّينِ﴾ with there being maad after the م. The rest recited it without maad. Refer to the book Huja Al-Qirat page 77.

world, from the vastness of one's sovereignty and control, command and prohibitions and obedience that is rendered to him and what occurs within that from the various types of awe and favors that are bestowed from the likes of this they still fall short in that no matter what they may reach from being masters and true kings. Here Allah said:

﴿مَالِكِ يَوْمِ الدِّينِ﴾

"The Owner of the Day of Recompense."

Thus He owns it, it being under His control. He is also the king, Majestic and High be He, upon that day. So His statement here, "The Owner..." in this contains cognizance of this meaning and it that everything upon that day is owned by Him, Glorified be He. And the meaning is that it all returns to Him and He manages it. And His command is administered within it and no one else manages anything upon that day nor can anything occur except after His permission. Thus, if anyone's heart is attached to other than Allah from the righteous, the prophets and false deities which are worshiped that they hope intercession from, Allah, the Mighty and Majestic, said regarding mention of the Day of Judgment:

﴿يَوْمَ لَا تَمْلِكُ نَفْسٌ لِّنَفْسٍ شَيْـًٔا ۖ وَالْأَمْرُ يَوْمَئِذٍ لِّلَّهِ ١٩﴾

"It is the Day when no one owns any power (to do anything) for any other soul. And the affair will (only) be with Allāh (with none to contend with Him)." (Al-Infitar 82:19)

And the statement of Allah here, "No one owns..." means no soul can do anything for another and no one can benefit someone else nor can anyone repel harm from someone else. The king and the Owner of all of this is Allah, the Mighty and Majestic. Allah then says:

﴿وَالْأَمْرُ يَوْمَئِذٍ لِّلَّهِ﴾

"And the affair on that Day belongs to Allah."

This contains attaching one's heart to Allah, the Mighty and Majestic, Alone; because these people had hope that those objects can intercede for them and bring them near to Allah. Yet, all of that is false by way of the statement of Allah:

﴿مَالِكِ يَوْمِ الدِّينِ ۝٤﴾

"The Owner of the Day of Recompense."
(Al-Fatihah 1:4)[1]

❁❁❁

[1] Refer to Tafsir Surah Al-Fatihah by Imam Ad-Da'wah within Majmu' Mu'alafat Ash-Shaykh Muhammad ibn Abdul Wahhab (2/32-33)

The Meaning of Ad-Deen in the Arabic Language and the Legislation

Within his statement. **"... the day of Ad-Deen,"** the word comes within the Qur'an bearing various meanings. Its origin in the Arabic language is a repetitive habit. The poet said:

«تَقُولُ إِذَا دَرَأْتُ لَهَا وَضِينِي... أَهَذَا دِينُهُ أَبَدًا وَدِينِي»

"You say when you repel it, wa Dini..., Is this his religion forever and my religion?"

Due to this Shaykh Al-Islam ibn Taymiyyah (رَحِمَهُ ٱللَّهُ) mentioned within a principle regarding the meaning of ad-deen: that the origin of ad-deen in the Arabic language is the repetitive habit. This speech is correct and corresponds with that of the scholars of the Arabic language. Thus, that which the person places within his heart from creed or with that which he places upon his tongue from statements or that which he does with his limbs from acts of worship, all of this is referred to as deen because he does it in a manner as though it is a repetitive habit because the deen is something that is done repeatedly. This is one of its interpretations. Therefore, what is intended by ad-deen is that which the person holds fast to from creed, statements, or actions. As Allah has said:

﴿إِنَّ الدِّينَ عِندَ اللَّهِ الْإِسْلَامُ﴾

"Indeed, the religion (ad-deen) in the sight of Allah is Islam." (Ali-Imran 3:19)

Also ad-deen is applied bearing the meaning of recompense. This comes in several verses. Amongst them there is the statement of Allah:

﴿مَالِكِ يَوْمِ الدِّينِ ﴿٤﴾﴾

"The Owner of the Day of Recompense." (Al-Fatihah 1:4)

From them as well is the statement of Allah the Exalted:

﴿يَوْمَئِذٍ يُوَفِّيهِمُ اللَّهُ دِينَهُمُ الْحَقَّ﴾

"That Day, Allah will pay them in full their deserved recompense." (An-Nur 24:25)

Meaning, their true reward. Therefore, ad-deen comes within the Qur'an bearing the meaning of reward or recompense in many verses. From that as well is the statement of Allah the Exalted:

﴿كَلَّا بَلْ تُكَذِّبُونَ بِالدِّينِ ﴿٩﴾﴾

"Nay, but you deny the (Day of) Reckoning and Recompense." (Al-Infitar 82:9)

Meaning, you deny the reward. Likewise, there is the statement of Allah, the Exalted:

﴿فَلَوْلَآ إِن كُنتُمْ غَيْرَ مَدِينِينَ ﴿٨٦﴾﴾

"Then why do you not, if you are not to be recompensed." (Al-Waqiah 56:86)

Meaning, not rewarded for your actions nor called to account.[1] There is a connection between it having the meaning of recompense and the linguistic origin which is that which is done repeatedly. In connection between the two meanings is that the recompense is repeated with the repetition of the action. Thus, the repetitious recompense is applied if its origin is done repeatedly and is variant.

✿✿✿

[1] Tafsir At-Tabari (1/157).

The Day of Ad-Deen is From the Names of the Day of Judgement

Allah said:

﴿مَالِكِ يَوْمِ الدِّينِ ﴾

"The Owner of the Day of Recompense."
(Al-Fatihah 1:4)

And this is the Day of Recompense and reckoning. The day of ad-deen is from the names of the Day of judgement and the Day of Judgement has many names within the Qur'an that are well known. Allah said: **"The Day of Ad-Deen,"** meaning, the Day of Judgement. What is intended from it is:

﴿يَوْمَ يَقُومُ النَّاسُ لِرَبِّ الْعَالَمِينَ ﴾

"The Day when mankind will (arise from their graves and) stand before the Lord of the Worlds."
(Al-Mutaffifin 83:6)

This is along with the fact that Al-Qiyamah includes everything between the first blowing of the trumpet to the entrance of the people of Paradise into Paradise and the people of fire into the Fire. All of this is the Day of Judgement from the first blowing to the second blowing and that which comes after it until the entrance of the people of Paradise into Paradise and the people of fire into the Fire. All of that which occurs, therefore, the master of all of that is Allah, the Majestic and High. As Allah, the Majestic and High has said:

﴿يَوْمَ هُم بَارِزُونَ ۖ لَا يَخْفَىٰ عَلَى اللَّهِ مِنْهُمْ شَيْءٌ ۚ لِّمَنِ الْمُلْكُ الْيَوْمَ ۖ لِلَّهِ الْوَاحِدِ الْقَهَّارِ ﴿١٦﴾﴾

"To whom belongs [all] sovereignty this Day? To Allah, the One, the Prevailing. This Day every soul will be recompensed for what it earned. No injustice today! Indeed, Allah is swift in account."

(Ghafir 40:16-17)[1]

Since the affair is like this, His statement here: **"The Owner of the Day of Recompense,"** means the day of reckoning and reward. And this is the day whereupon the people will stand before the lord of all that exists. Meaning, when they arrive at the land of gathering the dominion upon that day will be for Allah alone having no partners in that. Although, what is before is the dominion of Allah as well without doubt. Allah is the master of the dunya as well as the hereafter. And the master of that which is before the first blowing of the trumpet and that which is after it and that which is before the second blowing and that which is after it.

✿✿✿

[1] Refer to Tafsir ibn Kathir (1/134)

The Benefit of Specifying the Day of Recompense

The Day of Recompense is the day of reward and the day of reckoning. It is the day whereupon every soul shall be paid in full with that which it has done. And this is that which the souls cling to. Since the affair is like this then he who is the master on the day whereupon the doer of action shall be paid his wages in full thus, bringing about a connection to him from the standpoint of him looking towards that day then he will combine within his heart between looking in the dunya and love of Him, worshiping Him in the dunya and the connection of his heart to the hereafter. So therefore, if this is done repeatedly, then he bears in mind this affair.

Similarly, from the reasons for specifically mentioning that Allah is the master of the Day of Recompense in a place wherein the heart of the believing servant is present while he is reciting this verse of that which occurs on the Day of Recompense from the affairs in their entirety because Allah has said that He is the master of the Day of Recompense and the day whereupon all of those affairs will occur from the rising of the people from their grave, or from the people arriving to the gathering place and other than that until the people of Paradise enter paradise and the people of the fire enter the fire so it is as if the one who contemplates and reflects when he recites this bears all of these affairs in mind. And this will bring about constant fear other than the fear which would be brought about by mere mention that He is the master. This brings about benefit in the explanation of His statement:

﴿إِيَّاكَ نَعْبُدُ وَإِيَّاكَ نَسْتَعِينُ ۝٥﴾

"It is You alone (O Allāh) that we worship and it is You alone that we ask for help." (Al-Fatihah 1:5)

And this is the objective behind understanding and contemplation upon this and thus the objective will have been reached because the messengers were sent to guide the people to worship of Allah alone, to the exclusion of other than Him.

✪✪✪

The Meaning of: "You Alone We Worship"

Allah said, "You alone we worship..." so in the beginning one praises Allah with various types of praise then says, "You alone we worship." This is the first verb mentioned within the Quran and the first command mentioned within the Qur'an is:

﴿يَا أَيُّهَا النَّاسُ اعْبُدُوا رَبَّكُمُ الَّذِي خَلَقَكُمْ وَالَّذِينَ مِن قَبْلِكُمْ لَعَلَّكُمْ تَتَّقُونَ ﴿٢١﴾﴾

"O mankind! Worship your Lord (alone), who created you and those before you so that you may become pious." (Al-Baqarah 2:21)

Worship is what is intended in this instance because the contention occurred only in worship of Allah, the Majestic and High. Therefore, the servants worship their lord alone without associating anything as a partner with Him nor making shirk with Him.

Why does the statement, "You alone we worship," come after what has preceded?

The Response: The people of knowledge say that this is because worship has three pillars and when one performs all of them together, worship is present legislatively. Those three pillars are love, fear, and hope.[1] Therefore, worship is only established if the heart contains love, hope and fear. Have you not seen the worshiper for example when he prays he is bearing in mind the love that he has for his lord and the hope that he has in Him, the Majestic and High. (Hoping) that He should accept his worship and reward him for it. He bears in mind the fear that he has of Him, that He should punish him on the day of recompense if he were to abandon the prayers or be negligent within. Therefore, worship is only established by way of these three. Foundation of love, foundation of hope and the foundation of fear, if one of them is not present then worship is not present legislatively even though one is performing it. Here we draw attention to the fact that when one says:

﴿الْحَمْدُ لِلَّهِ رَبِّ الْعَالَمِينَ ۝٢﴾

"All praises be to Allāh, the Lord of all that exists."
(Al-Fatihah 1:2)

As we have mentioned it opens the door of love and when one says:

﴿الرَّحْمَٰنِ الرَّحِيمِ ۝٣﴾

---

[1] Refer to Madarij Al-Salikin (1/203).

"The Most-Merciful, the Bestower of Mercy." (Al-Fatihah 1:3)

It opens the door of hope and when one says:

﴿مَالِكِ يَوْمِ الدِّينِ ۝٤﴾

"Owner of the Day of Recompense." (Al-Fatihah 1:4)

It opens the door of fear. Therefore, the servant says: **"You alone we worship,"** if he comprehends this then within his heart he has established love, fear and hope. So from the mercy of Allah the Majestic and High upon the servant is that he turns to Him due to his statement: **"You alone we worship,"** while he is addressing his Lord, the Majestic and High, after having mentioned verses which invoke within his heart love, hope and fear in order that this statement of his can be in line with the legislation.

✪✪✪

The Benefit of Saying Iyyaka (You alone) Before Na'budu (we worship):

The scholars have stated that within this statement: **"You alone,"** coming before: **"We worship,"** that it is bringing the object of the verb which is the Damir (disconnected pronoun) before the verb itself. The origin is that the object of the verb comes after the verb itself. And here it comes before the verb and in bringing it ahead of the verb lies many benefits. From them it brings about restriction and limitation. This is something which is affirmed within the science of meanings and terminologies. Therefore, from the science of eloquence is the field of restriction and limitation.[1] Similarly, in the principles of

---

[1] Al-Qazwayni said within Al-Idaah (2/164): "Specification of something in most instances requires that it be mentioned first. Due to this it is said regarding the statement of Allah the Exalted:

﴿إِيَّاكَ نَعْبُدُ وَإِيَّاكَ نَسْتَعِينُ﴾

"It is You alone (O Allāh) that we worship and it is You alone that we ask for help." (Al-Fatihah 1:5)

fiqh is the field of opposite understandings.[1] The statement: **"You alone we worship,"** means we limit and restrict our worship to You. Some of the people of knowledge have said that it denotes specification. Meaning, we make our worship specific; and within the statement: **"You alone we worship,"** lies an indication towards tawheed al-ibaadah by way of clear mention of ibaadah.

✡✡✡

Its meaning is: We specify you with worship and we do not worship other than you. And we specify you with seeking aid and we do not seek aid with other than you. And within his statement:

﴿إِن كُنتُمْ إِيَّاهُ تَعْبُدُونَ﴾

"If it is [indeed] Him that you worship." (Al-Baqarah 2:172)

Its meaning is if you specify him with worship.

[1] Al-Tufi said with Shah Muktasir Al-Rawdah (2/724), "This is to specify something with a ruling that is indicated by the negation of that ruling from other than it and it is referred to as the opposite understanding such that we need to understand from it the opposite of that which has been stated." He mentioned an example of that in (2/754) mentioning the statement of Allah the Exalted: **"You alone we worship,"** meaning, we do not worship any other than the one (mentioned) before the verb **'we worship.'** From that as well is the statement of Allah the Exalted:

﴿لَا يَسْبِقُونَهُ بِالْقَوْلِ﴾

"They cannot precede Him in word." (Al-Anbiya 21:28)

Meaning, they do not act except by his command."

The Meaning of Ibaadah (worship) in the Arabic Language and in the Legislation

Ibaadah in the Arabic language means humility and humbleness or humbleness alone. Due to this it is said: بعير معبد "The tamed camel" if the reins have been placed within its mouth and it has been singled out. Thus, it has come to be tamed alone.[1] From this as well is the statement, "Tarfaah in relation to it being tied up."[2] As the poet said:

«إِلَى أَنْ تَحَامَتْنِي العَشِيْرَةُ كُلُّهَا... وأُفْرِدْتُ إِفْرَادَ البَعِيْرِ المُعَبَّدِ»

"Until the entire clan protects me...; And I am alone like the lone nature of the camel that has been tamed."

It is also said: طريق معبد "The beaten path," if it has been made flat by the abundance of footsteps upon it and the

[1]Al-Jawhari said with As-Sihah: "At-Ta'bid refers to is At-Tadh'lil (humbleness). It is said: 'The path that has been laid flat, and the camel that has been tamed.' Meaning it has been subjugated by way of the reins being placed upon it."

[2] This line of poetry is within Sharh Al-Qasa'id As-Sab' At-Tiwal Al-Jahiliyat (pg.191)

abundance of hooves and travel upon it. From this as well is the statement of the poet in description of the she-camel:

«تُبَارِي عِتَاقاً نَاجِيَاتٍ وأَتْبَعَتْ... وظِيْفاً وظِيْفاً فَوْقَ مَوْرٍ مُعْبَّدِ»

"Free, you're indicated allowed to roam, being led,
Working over the path that has been trodden."[1]

Al-Mawl المول refers to the path that is trodden from the abundance of steps placed upon it.

The scholars have said that ibaadah within the legislation is the epitome of love along with the epitome of humility and Ibn Al-Qayyim (رَحِمَهُ ٱللَّهُ) has mentioned it within Nuniyyah.[2] Other than him has mentioned it as well. Shaykh Al-Islam Ahmad ibn Taymiyyah (رَحِمَهُ ٱللَّهُ) defined worship as being: A comprehensive term for everything that Allah loves and is pleased with from statements and actions, both apparent and hidden.[3] As for the scholars of Usul, they define worship as being that which is commanded legislatively without there being room for custom nor

---

[1] See the line of poetry within Sharh Al-Qasa'id As-Sab' At-Tiwal Al-Jahiliyat (page 151). As well as *Lisan Al-Arab,* the definition of *Mawl.* (5/186). As well as Ad-Dur Al-Masun (1/57)

[2] Ibn Al-Qayyim mentioned within *Al-Kafiyah As-Shafiyah* page 64:

وَعِبَادَةُ الرَّحْمَنِ غَايَةُ حُبِّهِ... مَعَ ذِلِّ عَابِدِهِ هُمَا قُطْبَانِ...

وَعَلَيْهِمَا فُلْكُ الْعِبَادَةِ دَائِرٌ... مَا دَارَ حَتَّى قَامَتِ الْقُطْبَانِ...

"The worship of Ar-Rahman is the epitome of loving Him...
Along with the servant being humble, they are two pillars...
Upon them is the flow of worship, perpetual...
And it would not be established until its two pillars are established."

[3] Refer to Majmu' Al-Fatawa (10/149) as well as Fat'h Al-Majid Sharh Kitabul-Tawheed page 13.

intellect.[1] And all of these meanings are correct and truthful in relation to worship. Therefore, the statement: **"You alone we worship,"** means: *We single You out with worship to the exclusion of other than You and we do not worship other than You.* In this lies tawheed Al-Ibaadah, as is clear.

Therefore, the mushirk who associates partners with Allah and worships alongside Him other than Him when he says: **"You alone we worship,"** is he truthful or is he lying? Without doubt he is lying. Due to this the disbelievers and the polytheists are the biggest liars upon Allah, the Majestic and High, and the biggest liars upon themselves. Due to this, Allah the Exalted said within surah Al-An'am:

﴿انظُرْ كَيْفَ كَذَبُوا عَلَىٰ أَنفُسِهِمْ ۚ﴾

"See how they will lie about themselves."
(Al-An'am 6:24)

For he associates partners with Allah and along with this he says within his prayer: **"You alone we worship,".** You worship and supplicate to other than Allah, you slaughter for other than Allah, you seek salvation from other than Allah; how do you not understand the meaning of: **"You alone we worship"?.** This is from the greatest calamities; that one claims connection to the Qur'an, or Al-Fatihah, or the statement of Tawheed or the testimony that Muhammad is the messenger of Allah, yet, he is prevented from understanding its meaning to the point that one who speaks the Arabic language does not understand the meaning of that which he says or that which he hears from

[1] Ar-Rawdah Al-Muwabah (1/9) and Kishaf Al-Quna' (1/85 and 418)

the Qur'an. One says: **"You alone we worship,"** this contains singling out Allah with divinity.

❖❖❖

The Meaning of: "You Alone We Ask for Help"

This verse contains singling out Allah, the Majestic and High, with Al-Isti'anah (seeking help). The scholars have said Al-Isti'anah is brought later in the verse even though aid is something sought from the Lord, thus it returns back to the meaning of lordship. So, one says:

﴿إِيَّاكَ نَعْبُدُ وَإِيَّاكَ نَسْتَعِينُ ۝٥﴾

"It is You alone (O Allāh) that we worship and it is You alone that we ask for help." (Al-Fatihah 1:5)

For an appropriate reason and a tremendous goal and this is because the person of tawheed who says: **"You alone we worship,"** it is not possible for him to single out Allah in worship unless he seeks help from Allah alone in doing so. Otherwise, the Shayateen will seek to thwart and lead him astray.

Here one says: **"You alone we worship, you alone we ask for help,"** in one verse, the two statements being joined by way of a و meaning, you alone we worship. Therefore, we do not worship except you alone to the exclusion of other than you and you alone we ask for help in all of our affairs and we specify you with our worship alone to the exclusion of other than you. This makes the person of tawheed aware of the need that he has for his Lord in making him firm upon his tawheed because it is not possible to be firm upon the tawheed of Allah except by way of help from Allah. Therefore, when a servant says within his prayer: **"And you alone we ask for help,"** every notion of self-amazement departs and every notion of reliance upon oneself leaves and the servant is fully devoted and his heart is purified of the idea that he is not in need of Allah or that he can do without him for the twinkling of an eye. Yes, singling out Allah, the Mighty and Majestic, in worship and singling Him out in seeking of aid is in all of the affairs and it contains a great subtlety; and a great affair. He who actualizes it will have actualized the greatest of goodness.

The Meaning of: "Guide us to the Straight Path"

Allah the Majestic and High said thereafter:

﴿اهْدِنَا الصِّرَاطَ الْمُسْتَقِيمَ ۝٦﴾

"Guide us to the straight path." (Al-Fatihah 1:6)

Meaning, guide us O Allah; and the statement: **'Guide us,'** is a supplication. It is a verbal command and the verbal command, as is affirmed, if it is rendered to one who is higher in status than the one who has given the command then it is a supplication. If it is from someone who is a peer then it is a petition and if it is from someone who is less than the one who issued the command then it is a command.[1] Therefore, the statement: **"Guide us to the straight way,"** from the mercy of Allah, the Majestic and High, is that He

---

[1] Al-Akhdari said within the text of As-Sulam:

«أَمْرٌ مَعَ اسْتِعْلاَ وَعَكْسُهُ دُعَا ... وَفِي التَّسَاوِي فَالْتِمَاسٌ وَقَعَا»

"A command along with highness to the one that is commanded is a supplication..., and when it is rendered to peers then it is a petition, unequivocally."

revealed these verses in order that we can supplicate with them; and guidance, as well, is being sought here from Allah, the Majestic and High.

✪✪✪

The Meaning of Guidance in the Language and the Legislation

The reality of guidance is that it is direction and instruction within the Arabic Language. هدى means he guided and directed. Guidance within the text of the Quran is of four types:[1]

The First: Firmly embedded guidance. Meaning, the guidance of Allah, the Majestic and High, for the creation to that which is beneficial for them naturally. This is like the statement of Allah the Exalted:

﴿قَالَ رَبُّنَا الَّذِي أَعْطَىٰ كُلَّ شَيْءٍ خَلْقَهُ ثُمَّ هَدَىٰ ۝٥٠﴾

He said, "Our Lord is He who gave each thing its form and then guided [it]." (Taha 20:50)

The Second: Guidance bearing the meaning of direction and indication to that which is beneficial from the affairs of

[1] Ar-Raghib Al-Asfahani mentioned these four types within Mufradat Alfaz Al-Qur'an under the definition of هدى (pg 536). See as well Tafsir At-Tabari (1/167 and 169) as well as Tafsir ibn Kathir (1/137).

the religion. The first is natural in that which is beneficial to the affairs of the dunya. This guidance and directive to that which is beneficial to the affairs of the religion is similar to the statement of Allah, the Exalted to his prophet Muhammad (صَلَّى اللَّهُ عَلَيْهِ وَسَلَّمَ):

﴿وَإِنَّكَ لَتَهْدِي إِلَىٰ صِرَاطٍ مُّسْتَقِيمٍ ۝٥٢﴾

"And indeed, [O Muhammad], you guide to a straight path." (Ash-Shura 42:52)

Likewise His statement:

﴿وَلِكُلِّ قَوْمٍ هَادٍ ۝٧﴾

"And Each people have their guide." (Ar-Ra'd 13:7)

Likewise the statement of Allah:

﴿ وَجَعَلْنَا مِنْهُمْ أَئِمَّةً يَهْدُونَ﴾

"**And We made from among them leaders guiding by Our command."** (As-Sajdah 32:24)

And the likes of this. This directive guidance and instruction the messengers possessed the ability to give, as do the scholars and the callers.

The Third: Guidance bearing the meaning of *at-Tawfeeq* which is specific to those who have been guided and that is the result of directives and guidance. Will it be accepted or not? It requires acceptance for it to have the effect of at-tawfeeq. Due to this, it is said the guidance of tawfeeq meaning, the result of the guidance that has preceded and that is the guidance of direction and instruction and this is similar to the statement of Allah the Exalted:

﴿إِنَّكَ لَا تَهْدِى مَنْ أَحْبَبْتَ وَلَـٰكِنَّ ٱللَّهَ يَهْدِى مَن يَشَآءُ ۚ﴾

"Indeed, [O Muhammad], you do not guide whom you like, but Allah guides whom He wills." (Al-Qasas 28:56)

Meaning, you do not give tawfeeq to those whom you love. However, Allah grants tawfeeq to whomever He wills. Likewise, there is the statement of Allah the Exalted:

﴿وَمَن يُؤْمِن بِٱللَّهِ يَهْدِ قَلْبَهُۥ ۚ﴾

"And whoever believes in Allah - He will guide his heart." (At-Taghabun 64:11)

The Fourth: This is the greatest and the most eminent type and it is the epitome of all types of guidance and it is guidance to the path of Paradise[1] and guidance to the path of the Fire. The guidance of the believers is to the path of Paradise as is in a statement of Allah the Exalted:

﴿وَٱلَّذِينَ قُتِلُوا۟ فِى سَبِيلِ ٱللَّهِ فَلَن يُضِلَّ أَعْمَـٰلَهُمْ ۝٤ سَيَهْدِيهِمْ وَيُصْلِحُ بَالَهُمْ﴾

"And those who are killed in the path of Allāh, then He would never cause their deeds to be lost. He will guide them (to Paradise) and rectify their condition (in this life and the next)." (Muhammad 47:4-5)

The scholars have said He, the Majestic and High said about them that they were killed, "Those who were killed in the path of Allah their efforts would not be wasted" this is in the hereafter whereas they were killed. Therefore, guidance is not guidance of the dunya. Rather, it is guidance

[1] Refer to Madarij As-Salikin (1/52)

of the hereafter. The scholars of tafsir said concerning the statement, "**And he will guide them,**" meaning, to the path of Paradise.[1] And we ask Allah Al-Karim for His bounty.

Likewise, there is guidance to the path of the fire. Allah the Exalted has said:

﴿فَاهْدُوهُمْ إِلَىٰ صِرَاطِ الْجَحِيمِ ﴿٢٣﴾﴾

"**Other than Allah, and guide them to the path of Hellfire.**" (As-Saffat 37:23)

And the refuge is with Allah. Allah said:

﴿وَجَعَلْنَاهُمْ أَئِمَّةً يَدْعُونَ إِلَى النَّارِ ۖ﴾

"**And We made them leaders inviting to the Fire.**" (Al-Qasas 28:41)

We ask Allah for security. These are four types. So when one says: **"The straight path,"** it is inclusive of three types. The second third and fourth based upon the explanation of each. As for the second it is the guidance of direction and indication. The servant says this after he has been guided. Meaning, after it had been clarified to him that he has been directed towards Al-Islam. So the one who is praying recites this verse and he is from the people of Islam. However, what enters into the statement of the supplicant when you say to your lord, "Guide us to the straight way" is direct us, guide us **upon** the straight path. The affairs of the straight path in its individual types and aspects are many. It is not possible to enumerate them. The scholars strive in understanding this. Each scholar directs and guides towards this issue

[1] Tafsir ibn Kathir (7/309)

which is from the issues of legislation that make up the straight path. So the statement of one who says: **"Guide us to the straight path,"** he is seeking from his lord to clarify for him and to guide him upon the various types and affairs of the straight path by way of its various types and individual aspects in their multiplicity. Due to this the supplicant says when he makes dua: *"O Allah show us the truth as truth and abide us with following of it and show us falsehood as falsehood and provide us with the avoidance of it."*[1]

The affairs of the straight path are variant. There are those things which are recommended, those things which are disliked, those which are obligatory in its various types, there are those things that are permissible, the affairs of knowledge of Allah, the affairs of knowledge of His rulings, various types of knowledge of the effects of His names and attributes within the creation, the affairs are many. It is not possible to enumerate them. So the one asking within his statement, **"Guide us..."** he has supplicated to his lord to clarify all of this to him and this is that which we are the most in need of. This is how we explain it. However, in addition to this we ask Allah, the Majestic and High to guide us by way of the second meaning, which is the guidance of tawfeeq and inspiration because indication and direction without tawfeeq nor inspiration nor being set straight from Allah is a proof against the servant and it is not a proof for him. Hence, when one says: **"Guide us to the straight way,"**

---

[1] Ibn Kathir mentioned it within his tafsir (7/309) in explanation of the statement of Allah the Exalted (Al-Baraqah 2:46) and he began speech regarding this with his statement, "Within the narrated supplication that comes..."

after having asked Allah, the Majestic and High for direction and guidance he is asking Allah, the Majestic and High to give him success in all aspects of the straight path. Explanation shall come regarding the straight path in'sha-Allah.

Likewise, the last meaning from the types of guidance when one says: "Guide us to the straight way," the straight way is of two types. There is the path of the dunya and the path of the hereafter. The sirat within the hereafter has a description. It is the platform that is atop the hellfire. It is sharper than a sword, it is thinner than a hair and on its two sides are hooks similar to thorns of Sa'dan and the likes of that from that which have come within the Sunnah.[1]

And Allah the Majestic and High said within surah Maryam:

﴿وَإِن مِّنكُمْ إِلَّا وَارِدُهَا﴾

"And there is none of you except he will come to it."
(Maryam 19:71)

Beneath the sirat; i.e., beneath the bridge is darkness. No one can see the path except one who has been given light by

[1] Refer to the description of the Sirat within Tafsir ibn Kathir (5/254) with the explanation of the statement of Allah the Exalted:

﴿وَإِن مِّنكُمْ إِلَّا وَارِدُهَا﴾

"And there is none of you except he will come to it." (Maryam 19:71)

way of which he is able to see. As the Prophet (صَلَّى ٱللَّهُ عَلَيْهِ وَسَلَّمَ) said within the authentic narration:[1]

«الظُّلْمَةِ دُونَ الجِسْرِ»

"Around the bridge (meaning the sirat) is darkness."

As for the disbelievers, they will be in darkness and they will not know where the Sirat is and the Hellfire will be brought forth as Allah says:

﴿وَجِاْيٓءَ يَوْمَئِذٍۭ بِجَهَنَّمَ﴾

"And on that day, Hellfire will be brought close." (Al-Fajr 89:23)

And it will have 70,000 reins;[2] it will be dragged and the Sirat shall be laid across it. Darkness will be placed all around it. The disbelievers will come stumbling about within, falling into it as one falls into a bed. This sirat is the path from the platform that leads to Paradise, it will be laid across the hellfire. From its descriptions is that it is thinner than a hair, sharper than a sword and around it is darkness. Therefore, who is the one that is guided? Due to the greatness of this affair the prophets will say:

---

[1] Reported by Muslim in his sahih in the book of Menstrual blood, chapter: *The Description of the Semen of the Man in that of a Woman and That the Child is Created from Their Fluid* (no.315) from the hadith of Thawban (رَضِيَ ٱللَّهُ عَنْهُ).

[2] Reported by Muslim in his sahih from the book of Paradise in the description of its bliss and people, chapter: *The Hell-Fire* may Allah protect us from it (no.2842) with the wording: **"The hell-fire will be brought upon that day having 70,000 reins and each reins will have 70,000 angels dragging it."**

«اللَّهُمَّ سَلِّمْ سَلِّمْ»

"O Allah, safety, safety!"[1]

They will stop in front of the sirat and each prophet will say: *"O Allah safety, safety, O Allah safety, safety."* Therefore, the affair is intense.

So the one who supplicates to his lord saying: **"Guide us to the straight path,"** bears in mind that path. Therefore, the path within the dunya is forgotten and his heart thinks about the path of the hereafter and he asks Allah to guide him and direct him and make him upright upon that path so that he is able to see it and pass over it with what Allah decrees for him of speed and swiftness.

In these are various types of supplications which if the servant were to say them he will be sufficed by way of them. Due to this the scholars say the most needed request that the servant makes of his lord is the statement: **"Guide us to the straight way."** From the mercy of Allah, the Majestic and High, upon his believing slaves is that they did not know how to beseech Him and supplicate to Him and then He made for them this chapter which contains this tremendous supplication which he was previously unaware of its status and greatness and the need that the servant has for it. None

[1] Reported by Al-Bukhari within his sahih within the book of Tawheed, chapter: The Statement of Allah the Exalted: [Some] faces, that Day, will be radiant, Looking at their Lord. (Al-Qiyamah 75:22-23) (no.7437) from the hadith of Abu Hurayrah (رَضِيَ اللَّهُ عَنْهُ). See as well Fat'h Al-Bari (13/421). As well as Ahmad within his musnad (13/144), (16/527) (no.10,906)

is aware of this except those who Allah, the Majestic and High grants success to and how few they are.

✡✡✡

Explanation of the Straight Path

Within the statement: **"Guide us to the straight path,"** the straight path is intended to mean the path within the dunya and the path within the hereafter. As for the path of the hereafter, I have mentioned to you its meaning. As for the path within the dunya the scholars of tafsir amongst the salaf have differed regarding its meaning. Some say the straight path is the Qur'an. Others say the straight path is Islam. Others say the straight path is the sunnah and yet, others say the straight path is following the Prophet (صَلَّى ٱللَّهُ عَلَيْهِ وَسَلَّمَ). The scholars such as Ibn Jarir[1] as well as Ibn Kathir[2] and Shaykh Al-Islam[3] and a group of others say that all of these statements lead to one thing; because who ever hold fast to the Qur'an has held fast to Islam, and has held fast to the sunnah and thus has followed the Prophet (صَلَّى ٱللَّهُ عَلَيْهِ وَسَلَّمَ).

[1] Within his tafsir entitled Jami' Al-Bayaan An Ta'wil Aya Al-Qur'an (1/172-175)
[2] Within his tafsir (1/137-138)
[3] Within Majmu' Al-Fatawa (4/39)

Hence, the servant is asking his lord to guide him to the straight path within the dunya. Meaning, for Him to guide him to Al-Islam and guide him to the Qur'an and guide him to the following of the Prophet (صَلَّى ٱللَّهُ عَلَيْهِ وَسَلَّمَ). And here we present a question that is known with the people of tafsir and it is that the servant is praying had already been guided to Al-Islam and guided to the Qur'an so why is he making this request: **"Guide us to the straight way,"?** Meaning, direct us and guide us to Al-Islam and direct us and guide us to the Qur'an, direct us and guide us to the Sunnah, direct us and guide us to the following of the Prophet (صَلَّى ٱللَّهُ عَلَيْهِ وَسَلَّمَ).[1] The response to this question is that the scholars have said this request is a request for firmness upon the straight path.[2] This is because the worshiper has already entered into Al-Islam. Therefore, he is asking for firmness upon it. This is well-known in relation to commands that the meaning of commanding something that has already been actualized is seeking firmness upon that thing. Allah the Exalted has said:

﴿يَا أَيُّهَا النَّبِيُّ اتَّقِ اللَّهَ﴾

"O Prophet, fear Allah" (Al-Ahzab 33:1)

Meaning, be firm upon the taqwa of Allah the Majestic and High. Likewise, Allah has said:

﴿يَا أَيُّهَا الَّذِينَ آمَنُوا آمِنُوا﴾

---

[1] Refer to the Tafsir of Ibn Kathir (1/139)

[2] Ibn Jarir said within his tafsir (1/165) the meaning of which is: "Its meaning is: Give us success to have firmness upon it, as is reported by Ibn Abbas."

"O you who have believed, believe." (An-Nisa 4:136)

Meaning be firm upon Iman.[1] Similar has been said by many of the people of knowledge; and this response must be looked at. That which is correct and more sound is the second view point and it is that the statement: **"Guide us to the straight way"** if its meaning is Al-Islam or Qur'an or the Sunnah or following of the Prophet (صَلَّى ٱللَّهُ عَلَيْهِ وَسَلَّمَ) then there are details to it and it is that the straight path is vast and within it are many affairs and details. Hence, Islam is built upon five pillars and it has branches. Similarly, Iman is built upon six pillars and has branches, affairs, creed statements and actions. Likewise, is Ihsan. It has one pillar and this one pillar also has branches and so on. Hence, the affairs of Al-Islam are variant.

The verses of Allah, the Majestic and High, within the Qur'an which contain information and their information is variant. Allah has informed us with many things in the Qur'an and the commands and prohibitions are likewise numerous. So when one makes this request he is asking Allah to direct him as I have mentioned to you previously to

---

[1] Ibn Kathir said within his Tafsir (2/434) in explaining this verse: "Allah the Exalted is commanding His believing servants with entering into all of the legislations of Iman, its branches, pillars and subsidiary matters. And this is not a command to actualize something that has already been actualized. Rather, it is from completion of something that has not yet been completed and affirming it making it firm and being continuous upon it. As the believer says within every prayer: '**Guide us to the straight way.**' Meaning, give us insight within it and increase us in guidance and make us firm upon it. Hence, He has commanded them with Iman in Him and His messenger."

give him success in being upon all of these affairs and this request is with all of that which enters and to the affairs of Al-Islam. Due to this there is no one who is free of need of making this request. The Prophets are in need of this request. So the Prophet (صَلَّى ٱللَّهُ عَلَيْهِ وَسَلَّمَ) used to recite this being in need of it and the companions, may Allah's pleasure be upon them recited them while they were in need of it. Every individual who recites this verse can ask Allah, the Majestic and High to guide him to the straight way bearing this meaning along with its details, its types and its individual aspects. Everyone has a need for this in proportion to his situation. So when one recites this verse he should not say: *I am from the people of guidance so why am I asking for guidance?* Because it is said to him: *You are in the greatest need and are in dire need of asking your lord to direct you towards the affairs of this straight path that is variant and to teach you and to make you understand it and to give you success to this within the dunya by way of holding fast to it.* Then, (you're asking) to give you the reward for it within the hereafter by making you to pass upon the Sirat safely. So every request that we are in need of is from the affairs of the straight path. What makes this clear is that the Sirat in the hereafter, no one will pass upon it safely except the one who has strong certainty. Likewise, the people will be light moving across the bridge with swiftness in proportion to the strength of their certainty in their firmness and knowledge of this straight path within the dunya. Thus, in proportion to one's knowledge of the path in the dunya and his firmness upon holding fast to it shall be his state and condition on the Day of Judgement. Due to this, the scholars have said within the dunya there are hooks affixed to the heart and they are similar to hooks of desires and doubts as Ibn Al-Qayyim (رَحِمَهُ ٱللَّهُ) has mentioned at the beginning of Al-Madarij.[1] He said: "When doubts or desires attach themselves to your heart, think about the statement of Allah the Exalted:

﴿اهْدِنَا الصِّرَاطَ الْمُسْتَقِيمَ﴾

"Guide us to the straight way,"

Those hooks which are attached to the two sides of the Sirat. Our Prophet (صَلَّى ٱللَّهُ عَلَيْهِ وَسَلَّمَ) said:

«فَنَاجٍ مُسَلَّمٌ وَنَاجٍ مَخْدُوشٌ وَمَكْدُوسٌ فِي نَارِ جَهَنَّمَ»

"There will be those who pass over it (meaning the Sirat) amongst them there are those who will be safe, amongst them there are those who will see some scratches. Amongst them there are those who will fall off of it and enter the fire."[2]

---

[1] Meaning Madarij Al-Salikin (1/52)

[2] This is a portion of the long hadith that is reported by Al-Bukhari within his sahih in the book of Tawheed, chapter: "*The statement of Allah the Exalted: [Some] faces, that Day, will be radiant, Looking at their Lord. (Al-Qiyamah 22-23)* (no.7439) from the Hadith of Abu Sa'id Al-Khudri (رَضِيَ ٱللَّهُ عَنْهُ) and the wording that is the point of reference is, "So some will be safe, after receiving scratches and some will fall into the fire of Hell." Refer to Fat'h Al-Bari (13/515) in the print of Dar As-Salafiyyah. It is likewise reported by Muslim in his Sahih in the book of Iman, chapter: *The Lowest of the People of Paradise in Station* (no.482) from the Hadith of Hudhayfah (رَضِيَ ٱللَّهُ عَنْهُ) in the wording of the point of reference is his statement, "*On the two sides of the Sirat are hooks affixed to it and they will snatch some people away. So, some will be safe after receiving scratches and others will fall into the fire of Hell.*"

Bear this in mind and you will be safe. So, in proportion to the hooks within the dunya then they are the hooks of doubts and desires. Those hooks shall be there if Allah, the Majestic and High does not forgive the person and overlook their shortcomings. We ask Allah, the Majestic and High for safety and security.

✡✡✡

Review of What Has Preceded

We have clarified the meaning of guidance within the statement of Allah: **"Guide us..."** and the fact that this guidance is to the straight path and that His statement: **"Guide us to the straight path,"** contains notice for the one who says this statement, recites this verse along with other than him from his believing brothers within this is notice that this chapter, Surah Al-Fatihah is an obligation within the prayer. Meaning, the obligatory prayers and within the congregational prayers because one says: **"Guide us..."** Hence, it is noticed that this only occurs for one who has others along with him. As for the supererogatory prayers, they follow on from this. And at times they are congregational and at other times they are not so. And if the ruling is between obligation or option then the obligation takes precedence in many affairs, as is known.[1]

The statement: "Guide us to the straight way," the scholars of the Arabic language are united upon the fact that the meaning of the Sirat is the clear and upright path, having no crookedness within it, having an abundance of

[1] Refer to Al'Lam Al-Muwaqi'in (3/50).

people who traverse upon it. Ibn Jarir At-Tabari (رَحِمَهُ ٱللَّهُ) has reported consensus regarding this.[1] And what attests to this is the statement of the poet who said:

«أميرُ الْمُؤْمِنِينَ عَلَى صِراطٍ ... إِذَا اعْوَجَّ الموارِدُ مُسْتَقِيمِ»

"The chief of the believers is upon a Sirat...; Although those who traverse upon it may waiver, he is straight."[2]

This is as has been stated by the scholars and it comes in detail along with legislative evidence within the Book and the Sunnah. I am referring to the meaning of As-Sirat. Ibn Al-Qayyim (رَحِمَهُ ٱللَّهُ) and others have brought all of this together where they said: "The Sirat cannot be called a straight path unless it contains certain characteristics. The first is that it is one in its means of reaching the objective. The second is that it is the shortest path and the most correct path by way of which one reaches the objective; and this is evidenced by the term *Al-Mustaqim* (straight). For that which is straight does not waiver. That which waivers is longer than that which is straight. This is evidenced by the statement of Allah: **"Al-Mustaqim (straight),"** which is a description for the Sirat as being the shortest path by way of which one reaches the objective. The meaning of that is that other than it from paths, they are divergent and deviant paths which will not bring one to his objective in a manner that is pleasing by the one who set up this path. Likewise, it cannot be called The Straight Path unless it is

[1] Within his tafsir (1/170).

[2] This has been stated by Jarir ibn Atiyah Al-Khatfi. This line of poetry is in Al-Muhtasib (1/43) and Tafsir ibn Kathir (1/137). As well as Lisan Al-Arab (3/459)

broad and can accommodate the abundance of those who traverse upon it. And this draws attention to the fact that the Sirat has an abundance of people who traverse upon it. And the one who traverses upon it even if he is alone in his time frame, he is not alone considering the abundance of those who traverse upon this path. Due to this He says thereafter:

﴿اهْدِنَا الصِّرَاطَ الْمُسْتَقِيمَ ۝٦ صِرَاطَ الَّذِينَ أَنْعَمْتَ عَلَيْهِمْ غَيْرِ الْمَغْضُوبِ عَلَيْهِمْ وَلَا الضَّالِّينَ ۝٧﴾

"Guide us to the straight path. The path of those upon whom You have bestowed favor, not of those who have evoked [Your] anger nor of those who went astray." (Al-Fatihah 1:6-7)

Hence, it is a path that has an abundance of traversers upon it even if a person on a particular day or in a particular time sees no one traversing upon except himself. For indeed this path is broad.[1] And many groups of the friends of Allah have traversed upon it as well as those who were obedient to Him and His messengers. Likewise, Allah the Majestic and High has said in description of Ibrahim (عَلَيْهِ السَّلَامُ):

﴿إِنَّ إِبْرَاهِيمَ كَانَ أُمَّةً﴾

"Indeed, Ibrahim (Abraham) was an Ummah (unto himself)." (An-Nahl 16:120)

[1] Within tafsir ibn Kathir (1/138) it comes on the authority of Jabir regarding the statement, "Guide us to the straight path" and he said it is Al-Islam and it is broader than that which is between the heavens and the Earth."

Hence, he was an ummah. Meaning, an imam whose example is followed in goodness.[1] The Imam of this da'wah, Shaykh Muhammad ibn Abdul Wahhab (رَحِمَهُ ٱللَّهُ) said that Allah's statement: **"Ummah"** means abundance along with the fact that he was an imam whose example is followed in goodness. Thus, he said regarding his explanation that Ibrahim was an ummah in order that the one who traverses upon the path will not be discouraged, by the small number of those who accompany him in traversing upon it.[2] Therefore, even if the believer did not find anyone supplicating with the supplication: **"Guide us to the straight way,"** yet he found along with him Prophets and Messengers of Allah (عَلَيْهِمُ ٱلسَّلَامُ) then this will be sufficient for him to have certainty. And it will be sufficient as a consolation for him. This is from the descriptions of the straight path. and the path is attributed to Allah, the Majestic and High, at times as is within the statement of Allah:

﴿إِنَّ رَبِّي عَلَىٰ صِرَاطٍ مُّسْتَقِيمٍ ٥٦﴾

"Indeed, my Lord is on a path [that is] straight."
(Hud 11:56)

And as is said: *The path of Allah.* It is at other times attached to those who traverse upon it as is within the statement of Allah the Exalted:

﴿صِرَاطَ الَّذِينَ أَنْعَمْتَ عَلَيْهِمْ﴾

[1] Refer to Tafsir ibn Kathir (4/610-611).

[2] Refer to Majmu' Mu'alafat As-Shakyh Muhammad Abdul Wahhab within the book, Fadl Al-Qur'an wat-Tafsir (2/181)

"The path of those upon whom You have bestowed favor..."

The first description is a reference to that One that has set it up and made it, and the second is in light of those who traverse upon it, and making it to be their path. Sufficient is this to bring ease to the believing slaves. Because if he looks at the fact that this path was set up and arranged being made to be a path that would lead to the truth and a path that was set up by Allah, the Majestic and High, and our lord the Majestic and High is upon the straight path and that those who traverse upon it are the best of the creation of Allah, this will bring about the greatest form of ease within his heart, certainty and relaxation. This has as you can see various types of benefits.

✡✡✡

Explanation of the statement of Allah, The Path of Those Upon Whom You Have Bestowed Your Grace

Allah, the Majestic and High, has said thereafter:

«صِرَاطَ الَّذِينَ أَنْعَمْتَ عَلَيْهِمْ»

The path of those upon whom You have bestowed favor,

This path which has been defined within the previous verse by way of His statement: **"Guide us to the straight path",** and it has been described as being straight. It has likewise been said that the statement: **"Guide us to the straight way",** is either due to it being something which is known, meaning it is the path that is well known. Or in order to clarify its reality and this is something which is abundant upon the Arabic language.

Then, he emphasized this and defined it further after its previous description by way of adding that which necessitates specification and restriction,[1] as is affirmed

[1] Madarij As-Salikin (1/59-60)

within its place in the sciences of the Arabic language, for he said: **"The path of those upon whom you have bestowed your grace."** Allah, the Majestic and High, has mentioned that it is the path and that it is straight and he went further in defining it as being the path of those whom Allah, the Majestic and High has conferred His favor upon. He said:

﴿اهْدِنَا الصِّرَاطَ الْمُسْتَقِيمَ ۝٦ صِرَاطَ الَّذِينَ أَنْعَمْتَ عَلَيْهِمْ﴾

"Guide us to the straight path. The path of those upon whom You have bestowed favor." (Al-Fatihah 1:6-7)

And this has a benefit within it; and it is that the path as it relates to its definition upon its reality may be obscured to many of the people. Meaning, what path is the truth? It is the path, it is the way upon which traverse upon those whom Allah has conferred His favor. Thus, this removes any ambiguity. Because amongst the people there are those who do not know the reality of a thing as it may be because he is in need of knowledge and in need of contemplation and derivation of evidence. However, if he looks at it from the perspective of those who traverse upon it he will come to know it in a better way. This is from the benefits of defining something after its definition has already been given.

Allah the Majestic and High has said:

﴿اهْدِنَا الصِّرَاطَ الْمُسْتَقِيمَ ۝٦﴾

"Guide us to the straight path."

This is the definition of it by way of his statement, "Guide us to the straight path." Meaning, that it is known in terms of its description and its reality is well known. And the statement thereafter:

﴿صِرَاطَ الَّذِينَ أَنْعَمْتَ عَلَيْهِمْ﴾

"The path of those whom upon you have conferred your favor."

If the servant did not know this reality as it was described initially when he said: **"Guide us to the straight way"**, then its reality is known by way of those who traverse upon it. So who is the one who traverses upon this path if there is ambiguity to it? It is the one that Allah has directed you towards; being one and not variant. He said: **"Those upon whom you have bestowed your favor."** And those whom Allah has bestowed His favor upon are the people of Taqwa; the people who have actualized Islam. Because Allah, the Majestic and High, clarified within Surah Al-Baqarah that many claim that they will enter into paradise amongst the various groups, religions and paths. Allah has said within Surah Al-Baqarah:

﴿وَقَالُوا لَن يَدْخُلَ الْجَنَّةَ إِلَّا مَن كَانَ هُودًا أَوْ نَصَارَىٰ ۗ﴾

And they say, "None will enter Paradise except one who is a Jew or a Christian." (Al-Baqarah 2:111)

Then He clarified the proof which he who deserves entrance into Paradise must bear and it is traversing upon the straight path. This is the goal which all those who traverse upon that path seek after and those who traverse upon this way hope to arrive at after the pleasure of Allah, the Majestic and High, and after His mercy. He said thereafter:

﴿تِلْكَ أَمَانِيُّهُمْ ۗ قُلْ هَاتُوا بُرْهَانَكُمْ إِن كُنتُمْ صَادِقِينَ ﴿١١١﴾ بَلَىٰ مَنْ أَسْلَمَ وَجْهَهُ لِلَّهِ وَهُوَ مُحْسِنٌ﴾

"That is [merely] their wishful thinking, Say, "Produce your proof, if you should be truthful." Nay [on the contrary], whoever submits his face in Islam to Allah while being a doer of good." (Al-Baqarah 2:111-112)

Meaning, nay, those who enter into Paradise are: **"Whoever submits his face in Islam to Allah while being a doer of good."**

Meaning, the one who has these two descriptions, he actualizes Islam and actualizes Ihsan in actions, statements and belief. Allah the Majestic and High likewise clarified within Surah An-Nisa' those whom Allah has conferred His favor upon in a specific manner. He, Glorified be He said:

﴿وَمَن يُطِعِ اللَّهَ وَالرَّسُولَ فَأُولَٰئِكَ مَعَ الَّذِينَ أَنْعَمَ اللَّهُ عَلَيْهِم مِّنَ النَّبِيِّينَ وَالصِّدِّيقِينَ وَالشُّهَدَاءِ وَالصَّالِحِينَ ۚ وَحَسُنَ أُولَٰئِكَ رَفِيقًا ﴿٦٩﴾ ذَٰلِكَ الْفَضْلُ مِنَ اللَّهِ ۚ وَكَفَىٰ بِاللَّهِ عَلِيمًا ﴿٧٠﴾﴾

"And whoever obeys Allah and the Messenger - those will be with the ones upon whom Allah has bestowed favor of the Prophets, the steadfast affirmers of truth, the martyrs and the righteous. And excellent are those as companions. That is the bounty from Allah, and sufficient is Allah as Knower." (An-Nisa 4:69-70)

Thus, He clarified that those whom Allah, the Majestic and High conferred His favor upon and those whom this path is ascribed to are those who traverse upon it, upon light and upon correct evidence from their lord. They are the Prophets, the truthful, the martyrs and the righteous. They are those whom Allah, the Majestic and High has conferred His favor upon.

So when the servant sees that the Prophets were such that this was their Sirat and when he sees that the martyrs who fought in order that the word of Allah be made uppermost in the path of Allah, this was their path; where he sees the truthful who spoke truthfully and they brought truth and they believed in it; so as it relates to their statement, they said the truth. And as it relates to their belief they did not have a belief system which contradicted reality. And they did not act in opposition to what was obligatory upon them; in reality, these are the truthful. Hence, if you do not see anyone then search for the truthful and follow the example of the righteous because there is no timeframe which is devoid of them. And there are those who are righteous with them and righteousness of the heart unites them as do upright beliefs; and upright statements unites their tongue and the various types of goodly speech and righteous actions, which is following the Sunnah. This will make clear to you that this path is such that there is no ambiguity in it at all. Allah, the Majestic and High, has said: **"The path of those upon whom you have bestowed your favor,"** And who are they? They are those who have obeyed Allah, the Majestic and High and have answered Him and His Messengers from amongst the followers of the Messengers and the leaders and imams of these people are the Messengers and Prophets of Allah (عَلَيۡهِمُ السَّلَامُ). Allah the Majestic and High has said:

﴿اهْدِنَا الصِّرَاطَ الْمُسْتَقِيمَ ۝٦ صِرَاطَ الَّذِينَ أَنْعَمْتَ عَلَيْهِمْ غَيْرِ الْمَغْضُوبِ عَلَيْهِمْ وَلَا الضَّالِّينَ ۝٧﴾

"Guide us to the straight path. The path of those upon whom You have bestowed favor, not of those who have evoked [Your] anger nor of those who went astray." (Al-Fatihah 1:6-7)

This contains an ascription of the bestowing of blessings to Allah and this is the point of attention. For they have traversed upon this path which Allah has ascribed to them with his statement: **"The path of those upon whom you have bestowed your favor, not the path of those who have earned your anger."** And in addition to the fact that He has ascribed the path to them within this place, He draws attention to the fact that their traversing upon this path is only by way of it being a favor of Allah upon them and it is not a virtue from their own selves. For he said: **"The path of those upon whom you have bestowed your favor."** This distances the heart from being deluded and from reliance upon one's self and believing that one has attained Istiqamah or firmness upon it or will be firm upon it by way of his own efforts and hard work. Rather, the servant cannot do without Allah for the twinkling of an eye. Hence, the one who traverses upon this path does not traverse upon it except by way of the favor of Allah. Thus, He is the one who has guided towards the straight path and the straight path which he has guided towards is the path which he has blessed those who traverse upon it. Meaning, He has given them success to be upon it. So the beginning of the affair is from Allah and its ending to Allah and Allah the Majestic and High thereafter will reward those who invoke Him upon this path. And this is the greatest mercy and ennoblement, and blessing and kindness and bounty. He directs towards it and He gives success to be upon it. He guides to it and thereafter He rewards the servant. He is the one who has conferred favor and bounty. Without doubt this fills the heart with love upon love and total reliance upon Him and relegation of one's affair to Him. And inspiration for the soul to fulfill His rights.

✡✡✡

Review of That Which Has Preceded

Therefore, the Fatihah is a tremendous surah which contains foundations of creed and foundations of manners and legislative rulings. Due to this it is referred to as Umm Al-Quran and Allah has said:

﴿وَلَقَدْ آتَيْنَاكَ سَبْعًا مِّنَ الْمَثَانِي وَالْقُرْآنَ الْعَظِيمَ ﴿٨٧﴾﴾

"And We have certainly given you, [O Muhammad], seven of the often repeated [verses] and the great Qur'an." (Al-Hijr 15:87)

And this is the tremendous Quran and it is the seven often recited verses and it is the mother of the book and it contains within tremendous principles. Allah has said: **"The path of those upon whom you have bestowed your favor."** Their path is one. As for other than them, they are upon various paths, as has come within the Qur'an, and as is said regarding them they are upon divergent paths. However, they are paths that would not lead towards uprightness. Or they are paths that are not even a path at all. As Allah has said:

﴿وَأَنَّ هَٰذَا صِرَاطِي مُسْتَقِيمًا فَاتَّبِعُوهُ ۖ وَلَا تَتَّبِعُوا السُّبُلَ فَتَفَرَّقَ بِكُمْ عَن سَبِيلِهِ ۚ ذَٰلِكُمْ وَصَّاكُم بِهِ لَعَلَّكُمْ تَتَّقُونَ ﴿١٥٣﴾﴾

"And, [moreover], this is My path, which is straight, so follow it; and do not follow [other] ways, for you will be separated from His way. This has He instructed you that you may become righteous." (Al-An'am 6:153)

Therefore, the path is the path of Allah and other than this path there are Subul (ways) and upon each one of them there is a Shaytan calling the people towards that evil. There is no restriction to them nor a specific number. They are as divergent and multiple and as the timeframes and places. However, the path of Allah is one. He has attached it to Himself in order that you may know it; and he has likewise attached it to those who traversed upon it from His Awliya' in order that you may know. And he clarified as well that by way of which this path can be known and it is that it is different from the path of those that are destroyed.

✿✿✿

The Meaning of "Not the Way of Those Who Have Earned Your Anger"

Meaning: *The path of those upon You have conferred your favor is not the path of those who have earned Your anger.* As is the preponderant view regarding this verse according to a group of the people of tafsir.[1] Some of the scholars have said that the phrase, *ghair* (not) here is an exception.[2] Hence, similar to the phrase *hashah* (Allah forbid) and the phrase *kalla* (nay). Such as the statement: "The men entered غير Muhammad (not Muhammad)." Meaning they all entered with the exception of Muhammad (ﷺ). Thus it denotes exception. They say that the statement, ***"Not the way of those who have earned your anger,"*** is a disconnection

[1] Ibn Kathir said within his tafsir (1/140) regarding the statement of Allah, "The path of those upon whom you have conferred your favor." This is an explanation of the straight path and it is another term used to describe it according to the linguists and it is likely that it is also joined to it by a conjunction as an explanation.

[2] There is a rare recitation of this word, being accusative, thus having a fat'hah upon the رَ.

from that which has preceded.[1] Meaning, when one says: **"Guide us to the straight way, the way of those upon whom you have bestowed your grace, not the way of those upon whom is your anger."** The path of those upon whom Allah has conferred His anger and the path of those who have gone astray is not the path that we want nor do we desire it or choose it. This viewpoint needs to be reviewed linguistically. As well as from the standpoint of the meaning that is affirmed here. That which is most correct is the first view as the verifiers have affirmed and it is that the phrase ghair is an adjective[2] to that which has preceded it. And the phrase, **"Not the path of those upon whom have earned your anger,"** here, based upon this latent phrase, do they have their own path or are there variant paths for them? The

---

[1] Ibn Kathir said within his tafsir (1/140), "Some of the linguists claim that the term ghair here is an exception. Thus, it is disconnected from those upon whom Allah has bestowed his grace and they are not from them.

[2] It is said that the term ghair is a badal (another word used to describe) those. Thus, it is a badal that is indefinite in exchange for something that is definite. It has also been said that it is an adjective for those. Some deem this viewpoint to be problematic because the term ghair and the phrase those are both definite and thus it is binding that the adjective corresponds to the noun that it qualifies in being definite or indefinite. The response of this is from two angles. The first is that the phrase ghair here is definite by position because it occurs between two opposites. Hence, the path of those whom Allah's anger is upon it is the opposite of the path of those upon whom He has conferred His favor. Thus, it denotes that it is not from the same genus. Due to this the term ghair is definite by position. The second is that the relative pronoun *al-lathinaa* is resemblant to indefinite nouns and its vagueness. Thus, it is dealt with as indefinite nouns are dealt with. Refer to Ad-Dur Al-Masun (1/71).

response is that there is a difference regarding this issue; as it is the case that the term Sirat is used when something is praiseworthy. Whereas, Sabil is used for that which is blameworthy. Or is it the case that both terms can be used for something praiseworthy and something blameworthy?. This is a linguistic difference of opinion. Likewise, it is rooted in legislative usage. Based upon this, we say the meaning is not the Sirat, if the Sirat is used to denote something being praiseworthy and blameworthy. Or it is attached to the meaning of not the sabil. Meaning, the sabil of those who have earned your anger nor of those who have gone astray because when a term is omitted then it is correct that the term itself be understood in meaning or its meaning is implied if the wording is not suitable. This is a principle which is useful for you in latent phrases in the field of tafsir and other than it.

✿✿✿

The Meaning of: "Not the Path of Those Who Have Earned Your Anger Nor Those Who Have Gone Astray"

Those who have earned the anger of Allah are the Jews and those who have gone astray are the Christians. What attests to this is the hadith from the Messenger of Allah (صَلَّى ٱللَّهُ عَلَيْهِ وَسَلَّمَ) as is reported by At-Tirmidhi and others.[1] The scholars of tafsir have reported agreement regarding this. Hence, those who have earned the anger are the Jews because Allah, the Majestic and High, has described them within the Qur'an as having earned anger in many verses. Such as, the statement of Allah the Exalted:

﴿فَبَآءُو بِغَضَبٍ عَلَىٰ غَضَبٍۚ﴾

[1] It is within the musnad of Imam Ahmad (32/124)(no.19,381) from the hadith regarding the Islam of Adi ibn Hajm. Within it the Prophet (صَلَّى ٱللَّهُ عَلَيْهِ وَسَلَّمَ) said, "Those who have earned the anger are the Jews and those who have gone astray are the Christians." It is likewise reported by At-Tirmidhi within his jami' in the book of the tafsir of the Quran from the Messenger of Allah (صَلَّى ٱللَّهُ عَلَيْهِ وَسَلَّمَ) chapter that which has come within surah Fatihah (no.2954).

"So they returned having [earned] wrath upon wrath." (Al-Baqarah 2:90)

And likewise, the statement of Allah the Exalted:

﴿وَغَضِبَ اللَّهُ عَلَيْهِمْ﴾

"Allāh has become angry with them." (Al-Fath 48:6)

And the likes of this. They are in addition to having earned the anger of Allah went astray as well. Why did He describe the Christians with misguidance since they have also earned the anger of Allah? And He described the Jews with having earned His anger even though they are astray as well. The response, the scholars have stated that this is because the most specific of the characteristics of the Jews is that they have earned Allah's anger and because the most specific characteristics of the Christians is that they went astray.[1] Hence, both groups are described with the most specific characteristics that are attributable to them. The

---

[1] Ibn Kathir said within his tafsir (1/141), "The Jews did not do action and the Christians abandoned knowledge, Due to this, the anger is for the Jews and misguidance is for the Christians because the one who knows yet abandons that knowledge is deserving of anger in opposition of the one who does not know. Whereas, the Christians intended one thing, however, they were not guided to the path of its attainment because they did not come to its proper door which is following the Messenger (صَلَّىٱللَّهُعَلَيْهِوَسَلَّمَ). Thus, they went astray. And both groups, the Jews and the Christians are astray and they have earned Allah's anger. However, the most specific of the characteristics of the Jews is them having earned Allah's anger. And the most specific of the characteristics of the Christians is that they have gone astray. This has been mentioned in ahadith and narrations."

Jews went astray, however, their deviation was worse because they earned Allah's anger. The Christians went astray as Allah the Majestic and High has said concerning them:

﴿قُلْ يَا أَهْلَ الْكِتَابِ لَا تَغْلُوا فِي دِينِكُمْ غَيْرَ الْحَقِّ
وَلَا تَتَّبِعُوا أَهْوَاءَ قَوْمٍ قَدْ ضَلُّوا مِن قَبْلُ وَأَضَلُّوا كَثِيرًا
وَضَلُّوا عَن سَوَاءِ السَّبِيلِ ۝٧٧﴾

Say, "O People of the Scripture, do not exceed limits in your religion beyond the truth and do not follow the inclinations of a people who had gone astray before and misled many and have strayed from the soundness of the way." (Al-Ma'idah 5:77)

✿✿✿

The Definite Article Alif and Laam on the phrase 'Al-Maghdubi'

He said:

﴿غَيْرِ الْمَغْضُوبِ عَلَيْهِمْ﴾

Not the path of those who have earned your anger,

The scholars have stated that the term al-maghdub itself is an object of a verb and the definite article ا and ل come at its beginning. It is affirmed that if an object of a verb commences with ا and ل then it is a relative pronoun, as Ibn Malik stated within Al-Alfiyyah: *"A clear description commencing with* ا *and* ل *then it being a declinable verb is rare."* The meaning of the clear description is the doer of a verb and the object of a verb. Based upon this the statement of Allah the Exalted, **"Not the path of those who earned your anger"** is as if He is saying not those who you are angry with. This means that they are those who Allah is angry with much because He articulated this by way of the relative pronoun which is the definite article at its beginning or the definite article here is to restrict it, although it is relative. Meaning, it brings about definition based upon the chosen viewpoint of some of the linguists.[1] What is intended is that He is angry at the Jews. And the reason for this anger as the scholars have mentioned is that they had knowledge but opposed it. They had clear and evident knowledge and various proofs were established against them and they knew the truth, it was clear to them. However, they opposed it while being certain of it and knowledgeable of that. As Allah has said:

﴿ٱلَّذِينَ آتَيْنَاهُمُ ٱلْكِتَابَ يَعْرِفُونَهُ كَمَا يَعْرِفُونَ أَبْنَاءَهُمْ ۖ وَإِنَّ فَرِيقًا مِّنْهُمْ لَيَكْتُمُونَ ٱلْحَقَّ وَهُمْ يَعْلَمُونَ ﴿١٤٦﴾﴾

"Those to whom We gave the Scripture know him as they know their own sons. But indeed, a party of them conceal the truth while they know [it]." (Al-Baqarah 2:146)

They declared the halal to be haram knowing that it was halal. And they declared the haram to be halal knowing that it was haram and they changed the set limits of Allah knowing that they were the set limits of Allah, the Majestic and High. Thus, they were described as having earned Allah's anger and anger comes against the Jews in totality while those who did those actions were their scholars. This indicates, as a group of the people of knowledge have mentioned, that the majority of them followed their scholars in their rulings. This is an important issue and Allah, the Majestic and High said concerning the Christians: **"Nor those who have gone astray."** Meaning, not the path of

---

[1] This has been stated by Abul-Hasan Al-Akhfash and it is the second viewpoint of Al-Mazini. Refer to At-Tasrih bi-Madhmun At-Tawdih in the chapter of Relative Pronouns.

those who have gone astray and the phrase, “Ad-Dallin” is the sound plural of ad-Dall and ad-dal is the doer of misguidance, or it is a noun to denote the one who establishes misguidance.

✿✿✿

The Definition of Misguidance Linguistically and Legislatively

Ad-Dalal (misguidance) in the Arabic language means forgetfulness, as Allah, the Majestic and High, has said:

﴿أَن تَضِلَّ إِحْدَاهُمَا فَتُذَكِّرَ إِحْدَاهُمَا الْأُخْرَىٰ﴾

"So that if one of the women errs, then the other can remind her." (Al-Baqarah 2:282)

And Allah the Glorified has likewise said:

﴿وَقَالُوا أَإِذَا ضَلَلْنَا فِي الْأَرْضِ أَإِنَّا لَفِي خَلْقٍ جَدِيدٍ﴾

"And they say, "When we are lost within the earth, will we indeed be [recreated] in a new creation?" (As-Sajdah 32:10)

Meaning, they will occupy this position when their flesh and bones have gone into the earth; the position of one who is forgotten and separated to the point that they will not be something that is even mentioned. Thus, ad-Dalal means forgetfulness. Meaning, it is utilized to refer to one who has opposed the truth without knowledge, turning away from the truth not being aware of that. Thus, the connection between its linguistic meaning and its legislative meaning is clear. The phrase: **"Nor of those who have gone astray,"** refers to the Christians because they do acts of worship upon ignorance. They have gone astray and are not of those who intended this. Allah, the Majestic and High has clarified this within surah Al-Hadid wherein He said:

﴿وَرَهْبَانِيَّةً ابْتَدَعُوهَا مَا كَتَبْنَاهَا عَلَيْهِمْ إِلَّا ابْتِغَاءَ
رِضْوَانِ اللَّهِ فَمَا رَعَوْهَا حَقَّ﴾

> **"And monasticism, which they innovated; We did not prescribe it for them except [that they did so] seeking the approval of Allah. But they did not observe it with due observance."** (Al-Hadid 57:27)

This contains a warning from traversing upon these two paths in reality. The first path is the path of those who resemble the Jews. The second path is the path of those who resemble the Christians.

The people who recite this Fatihah in this ummah are either from the outright scholars or from those who are of their ilk from the students of knowledge or those who ascribe to knowledge or the likes. Or they are from those who worship but are not scholars nor are they from those who ascribe to knowledge. These two categories within this ummah from those who recite this Fatihah and who perpetually repeat it within their prayer and Allah, the Majestic and High, after mentioning the path, He mentioned the description by way of those who traverse upon it. And He mentioned that which distinguishes this path by mentioning those who are destroyed and they are those who had knowledge yet opposed the knowledge. And we ask

Allah for safety and security. And they are those who follow their desires and worship Allah upon ignorance.

✡✡✡

Surah Al-Fatihah Contains Dua

When this is clear, let us return back to the statement, **"Guide us to the straight way, the way of those upon whom you have bestowed your favor, not the way of those who have earned your anger nor of those who have gone astray".** Let us note that this is the Dua that Allah has revealed to guide His servants and to clarify this path to them. Thus, He alerts His servants within this Dua of theirs to what is befitting to be within their hearts. The supplicant when he supplicates thinks about that which he is supplicating with. So when he says: **"Guide us to the straight way,"** he is asking Allah for guidance to this Sirat and he is speaking as well with the description of the Sirat addressing his lord with that by saying: **"The path of those upon whom you have bestowed your favor."** The meaning of this is that he desires to traverse upon the path of those who have been favored. When he says: **"Not the way of those who have earned your anger nor of those who have gone astray,"** this means that he does not desire nor does he want to be close to it; nor does he want it. Rather, he seeks refuge with Allah from the path of those who have opposed based upon knowledge and from the path of those who worship based upon ignorance.

So you see that these verses bring about guidance for the heart from every angle such that if one contemplates upon this supplication as it should be contemplated upon, the pathways of Shaytan will be closed. And this is the path being referred to in the statement: **"Guide us to the straight path,"** and with it being attached to Allah and the need of the servant for guidance such that he asks for that his heart is consoled by the fact that he is along with those whom Allah has conferred His favor upon; and they are the people of obedience to Allah and obedience to His messenger and the people of taqwa. Then, his heart will be filled with hatred, a lack of desire and disdain for those who had knowledge but opposed that knowledge and those who worship upon ignorance. And these categories are abundant within this Ummah, I am referring to those who worship upon ignorance and those who know but abandon that knowledge in creed, in worship, in fiqh, in manners etc. Similarly, those who worship without insight.

Speech Regarding the Phrase: "Ameen"

Then it is legislated for the one who completes recitation of Al-Fatihah if he is within the prayer that he says thereafter: *Ameen.*[1] This is a verbal noun bearing the

---

[1] It is reported by Al-Bukhari within his sahih from the book of tafsir chapter, "*Not the Path of Those Who Have Earned Your Anger, Nor of Those Who Have Gone Astray*" (no.4475) from the hadith of Abu Hurayrah (رَضِيَ اللَّهُ عَنْهُ) that the Messenger of Allah (صَلَّى اللَّهُ عَلَيْهِ وَسَلَّمَ) said: ***"When the imam says: 'Not the path of those who have earned your anger nor of those who have gone astray' say Ameen. For he whose statement corresponds with that of the angels will have whatever has preceded of his sins to be forgiven."*** Refer to (no.781, 782 and 2402). Ibn Shihab said, "*And the Messenger of Allah (صَلَّى اللَّهُ عَلَيْهِ وَسَلَّمَ) would say Ameen.*" (no.780), Ibn Hajar said within Fat'h Al-Bari (2/262),:"The phrase Ameen has maad (is elongated) and it likewise is shortened within all of the recitations from all of the reciters. Al-Wahidi reported from Hamzah and Al-Kasa'i that he would lengthen it." And there are three other ways of reciting it that are rare, that of shortening, that of at-Tashdid (placing a shaddah upon the م along with elongation and that of shortening the kasra. And the phrase Ameen is from the verbal nouns. It begins with a hamza al-wasl because it is indeclinable by

meaning of, "*Respond.*" The phrase 'Ameen' is elongated and at times it is shortened and it is linguistically sound. The phrase: 'Ameen' is not a part of Al-Fatihah. However, it is a supplication bearing the meaning of: "Respond" and the one who says Ameen is one of the supplicants as well. Meaning, when the Imam recites Al-Fatihah he is supplicating with these supplications. Thus, after it the person says Ameen so it is as if he shares in the supplication. Meaning it is as if he said this Dua from its beginning to its end for himself and those that are with him. The evidence for this is the statement of Allah the Exalted in Surah Yunus:

﴿وَقَالَ مُوسَىٰ رَبَّنَا إِنَّكَ آتَيْتَ فِرْعَوْنَ وَمَلَأَهُ زِينَةً وَأَمْوَالًا فِي الْحَيَاةِ الدُّنْيَا رَبَّنَا لِيُضِلُّوا عَن سَبِيلِكَ ۖ رَبَّنَا اطْمِسْ عَلَىٰ أَمْوَالِهِمْ وَاشْدُدْ عَلَىٰ قُلُوبِهِمْ فَلَا يُؤْمِنُوا حَتَّىٰ يَرَوُا الْعَذَابَ الْأَلِيمَ ﴿٨٨﴾﴾

"And Moses said, "Our Lord, indeed You have given Pharaoh and his establishment splendor and wealth in the worldly life, our Lord, that they may lead [men] astray from Your way. Our Lord, obliterate their wealth and harden their hearts so that they will not

---

way of total agreement. Its meaning is: O Allah, accept it, according to the majority of the scholars. The Ta'min (saying Ameen) bears the meaning of abridgment of a longer idea. Therefore, the supplicant goes into detail regarding that which he intends when he says, **'You alone we worship, you alone we ask for help,'** up to its end. And the one who says Ameen encompasses all of that with one statement. Therefore, when the Imam says it, it is as if he had said the supplication twice. Once in detail and the other in brief. Al-Bayhaqi reported that when Ibn Umar would say the Ameen the people would say it along with him. And he held this is to be from the sunnah.

believe until they see the painful punishment." (Yunus 10:88)

Then, who is the one who supplicated with this dua? It was Musa. Then, Allah the Majestic and High said in the verse that comes after:

﴿قَالَ قَدْ أُجِيبَت دَّعْوَ﴾

"[Allah] said: The supplication of you two has been answered." (Yunus 10:89)

The scholars of tafsir say this is because Harun was saying Ameen after the supplication of Musa and the one who says Ameen is one of the two supplicants and it is as if he supplicated for himself and for his brother.[1] Due to this the one who does not say Ameen within his prayer has deprived himself of abundant good.

And may prayers and peace be upon our prophet Muhammad (ﷺ), his family, and his companions all together.

❁❁❁

[1] Refer to Tafsir Ibn Kathir (1/146-147).